the smallest stories
to *extra*ordinary

the smallest stories
to *extra*ordinary

Dr. Priya Virmani

PARTRIDGE

To order additional copies of this book, contact
Partridge India
000 800 10062 62
orders.india@partridgepublishing.com

www.partridgepublishing.com/india

For Papa
because of you I know love
the kind that endures

For Mama
for the unconditional

For my readers
the Joy and Hope, that make waters part
and come together again, lie in you

It is your light that lights the worlds –
Rumi

Acknowledgements

My daily life is epicentered to the rhythm of gratitude. The gratitude I feel is immeasurable and the people to thank are many – those who have inspired me in lifting me and, equally those who have taught me better by challenging me. It is in challenges that one witnesses an infinite and sagacious growth of the very spirit, the energy force, that shapes one's life.

Even for this book, there are many whose influences and stories, and experiences with me, have shaped me and sensitised me to sense what I have seen, to pen these stories. My gratitude is heartfelt.

Foremost, to my parents – knowing I can always re-turn is one of the most powerful knowings. And yet to know, you let me go too. Unconditional love I've learnt it is.

To all the books and writers that have 'shown' me perspective; to the music and mantras that have helped me know subtlety; to my meditation practice and my talks and workshops that have built me in spirit – I'm thankful each day.

To every protagonist in this book, though names are mostly changed to ensure anonymity[1] (in places I don't even know the names of the protagonists) the stories are testament to *your move of my heart*.

To my friends – each of you knows who you are – you are the family meant for me.

Graphics Que and Harshita for initially exploring cover design options with me. To Devang for being a great sounding board, for executing the cover design and bringing it into existence.

To Ronak, Niharika and Rutej – for making magnanimity not a word, but a series of actions – for your much valued feedback through the journey to birth this book.

To Vivek – your ways, time and again, reinstate my faith in humanity – and so, yours is the voice this book begins with.

To the Paint Our World children – for showing me, each time, the joy and power of transformation, of the light within us all.

To my readers – for your faith.

To the universe – for your abundance.

Is thank you a sufficient word? May my thank yous be best known in how I choose to live my life.

Contents

Foreword

I'm an actor. Why then am I writing this foreword? I'm writing it because I am an actor. And my first and most pivotal act, like that of each of us, is the act of being human. It's the most salient act to get right. Right? Because when we get this one act right we change the tenor of this gift called life for ourselves and for all of humanity – for the better.

Shakespeare said, 'All the world's a stage and all the men and women merely players'. But the one part that gets trampled in the process of our other role plays, is being human. Recognising that humanity within us, is a true sense of liberation in an otherwise materialistic world. The true key to happiness is becoming the creator of joy for others. When it emanates from within, you become joy itself. This collection of short stories swells gently and powerfully within us to lift us to this space of being human – of knowing, feeling and participating in the miracle of being human and of recognizing this miracle in those we meet and the lives we touch and uplift and vice versa.

My connect with this book begins with the beliefs I share with the writer and with her acts, and so with her written word. We both met and connected for a common cause – to do our bits, in our everyday lives to make life better for others and inevitably for ourselves. How does lifting the life of another have any benefit to ourselves, I hear some of you ask. Our little acts of kindness can create so much positive energy that they can cause a ripple effect to actually shift the energy of the world we live in. Moving from complaining to caring, from caring to healing and from healing to joy, is the most satisfying and empowering experience of life. Just a thought, if seven billion people did one, just one little selfless act of kindness a day, this world would transform into paradise! All you have to do, is practice one act of selfless kindness a day and you can change the world! Priya and my connect worked to this effect. I introduced her to the beautiful charity Food for Life Vrindavan where my Foundation has been running Project Devi for the last eleven years, rescuing girls from forced labour and child prostitution, empowering them out of exploitation using education and healthcare as our tools. Priya visited and conducted talks and workshops with the girls empowered by the charity who are very close to my heart and now, to hers too. It was beautiful to see her painting smiles on their faces with her boundless love and compassion. Priya is truly beautiful on the outside and within. She has discovered the key to the cycle of empowerment and it's quite simple actually. In empowering ourselves we are better placed to empower others and in empowering others we further empower ourselves in the most life affirming ways. Priya, in turn, has introduced me to Paint Our World – the children's charity she has founded that works to make our most invisible children invincible. With little, loving acts I have supported Priya's work with the 'Paint Our World' children. I vividly recall drowning in the midst of the black leather chairs of a conference room, when Priya's message arrived that 'the Paint Our World children are super eager to speak to [me]'. I briefly excused myself and stepped out of the meeting. Then made a video call to the children. The result was an abundance of smiles made possible by a simple gesture. The expressions of disbelief and then untempered glee I saw on their little faces, remains unforgettable. As Mother Teresa put it, 'Do little things but with great love,' and we see the colours of our world start changing. The fog of despair gives way to the spread of sunshine smiles.

The stories in this book are little stories – stories of the everyday, highlighting the extra in the ordinary – an 'extra'ordinary we often bypass because it's bigger things we are chasing after. Written in narratives that are richly wondrous and moving, the simplicity of the characters dazzles making them 'extra'ordinary. Bigger things often bring lesser love – this book makes you think about it. An endearing love for the protagonists, and what their stories symbolize, is a thread that runs through the unraveling of each story. In the process of travelling through these 'life snippets' we arrive at a vantage point of insights into our own lives. The magic lies in how each story is told such that it tenderly asks us to assess our choices – and shift to ones of greater joy and shows how this is achievable 'within' daily life. The question is, are you ready to make your life 'extra'ordinary? Then empower yourself, feel inspired by these little stories and don't despair with your struggles – know that you can transform them to become your angel wings.

Vivek Oberoi

Prologue

Life, what is it? Really? Philosophers, writers, thinkers, spiritualists, religious leaders and each of us at some points during our lives have asked this question of ourselves and others. We often ask this question in times of confusion and conflict; when we face heartbreak and loss; when our dreams get trampled on or our wings broken; and when we face injustice meted out to us, we inevitably ask – what is all this for? And why me? Yet the best of our human minds and intellect put together have never really been able to fully comprehend this conundrum called life. We have never as a species been able to completely decode the DNA of this conversation called life, that each of us is gifted with for a finite period of time. Perhaps we don't have the physiology to know the mysteries of life in totality. But what we do have is the sensibility to wonder at these mysteries and partake in them, for each of us is a part of this wondrous mystery. But when the humdrum of daily life, replete with its routine and expectations, takes over, we often forget this. This collection of stories culled from daily life, is a journey that gets you thinking – that takes you from the humdrum of the everyday to show you there is joy and empowerment in the everyday – no matter who you are and at what juncture you are in your life.

As humans we are innately complex beings. We are conditioned by our genes; our nurture; our experiences of relationships; our reconciliations with love; our fights with our desires; our surrender to letting go. We are trillions of cells in a dance. We are a brain neurochemistry. A mind; a soul; a body; a personality; a character; likes and dislikes; loves and hates; anger and reconciliation; war and peace. Then we have roles we play – friend, lover, mistress, child, adult, adolescent, parent, relative, victim, survivor, winner, loser, spouse to name a few. Professions are laid on that – doctor, engineer, surveyor, actor, teacher, artist, writer and the like. We have a past, 'are' a present and we are a 'process' of becoming – the future. Then we have the rules that society lays down on us (some societies more than others) – how we should love, who we should be, who we should love and till when. And the metrics of how this is measured. And yet, then, it all ends so simply. The whimpers of life die in the bang of silence. We return. To. Earth. Dust. Ashes – all of us, complex beings, contained in this simplicity.

I vividly recall how I felt holding the urn with my father's ashes. As I travelled with his ashes to lay them to rest my conversation with the urn brought home so cruelly, yet so peaceably and simply, the realisation of all that the ashes held – the pride and yearning in his eyes (he had come to visit me in the U.K. while I was studying and little did we know it would be our last meeting); the love in his heart; the tenor of his temperament; the thoughts in his mind; the dance in his feet; the concern in his expressions. His heart, his mind, his eyes, his expressions, his gesticulations, his hug had lapsed into dust. But the feeling of protectiveness in his hug; the embrace in his conversation; the meaning in his song; the love in his heart – all stayed back. They turned into memories in me, that I will hold and relay on, till my metamorphosis to dust comes. Hopefully then, I too will have passed on my existence in meaningful memories to those I have encountered and touched. Through this churn of life, life moves on, unabated. The show *does* go on.

The show – what really gives flesh and blood to the bones of this show? What shapes it into a journey? A journey that we are so attached to, yet one that is severed from us in inevitable death so absolutely, never to return. And not just in death but even in life, when traumatic happenings raise their ulgy head, we often experience the loss of a part of us – a part of us dies in life. Yet it is at such times of crisis, of 'death in life' that the turnaround to growth can best take shape. These are the junctures where powerful learning happens and wisdom takes shape to bring us to the recognition that it is from our caterpillar struggles that we grow our butterfly wings.

Each person's show is often shaped by the very unpredictabilities of life we seek to control. In a world that is innately uncertain, we try hard to orchestrate 'our show' to certainty. In a journey that is replete with insecurity, we seek security. And we deal with unpredictability by trying to engineer a life that is as predictable as possible. In the process, playing safe has become more sanctimonious than being real. Being pragmatic and immune is seen to carry greater benefits than being empathetic and vulnerable. Yet the richness of the human journey – the interim we get between cradle and ashes, between our first cry and last silence – the richness of it is best known in empathy and vulnerability. Strong in their tenderness, the vulnerability of the protagonists of these stories becomes a paean to life.

Vulnerability – our frontiers of it are tested the most by how we are treated by those we love, those who we give the permission to, to know the heart of our vulnerabilities, to know where it hurts most. And how. And how much. Yet the wisdom is to never let the shadows of others on you, or those of your circumstances, determine you. Despite all our work at certainty, at predictability, at security and most of all at the 'safety' of love – love does let us down and life does become difficult, really imperfect and messy. How then should you and can you, when everything around you seems tumbling down, return to centre?

The journey to equilibrium is imperfect, but equally, it is empowering and beautiful. Difficulties mostly arise in our mind, in our perception and this stems from how we are conditioned. From the space of this conditioning we pigeon–hole ourselves; limit ourselves into what we can do and what we can't because of how we will be perceived. When that conditioned 'you' is overcome by the authentic you – you become 'one' – the empowered one. And this journey is truly a celebration. It is where you discover defiance and acceptance in vulnerability, faith in uncertainty, humanity in insecurity, enthusiasm in unpredictability and the ability of life to surprise you as you journey through it. Each time you go through this process, inner resolve grows – the resolve to rise to your best authentic self despite all that surrounds you that might be weighing you down.

Authenticity, I've learnt, is the best coping strategy because you will emerge being true to yourself. But authenticity is often not received well in the societies we have created. In the words of James Baldwin, 'And they would not believe me precisely because they would know that what I said was true'. All the more it becomes imperative to trust our inner well or soul space which also becomes the space to retreat to for an energy recharge when we are misunderstood and our intentions questioned, and when we deal with difficult people and challenging situations. Is it the space where calm can be nurtured to be solid and deep because it is nurtured by the universal energy beating in you. That has brought you to life. It will take you through life. Meaningfully. As Rumi said, 'You are not a drop in the ocean but the entire ocean in a drop'.

This book will be a companion through your journey. It is replete with life affirming short stories taken from everyday life experiences with people I've encountered. I hope they will lift, delight and 'shift' you just as they did with me. They encapsulate the 'lift of life' that the everyday provides – that usually through the demands of the everyday, we overlook. Yes, in the same everyday that we often feel is buried in the monotony of routine and the stress of delivering, also lies joy – if only we are as conditioned to look for it as we are to dealing with our march to the 'big destinations' like the coveted house, job, car, partner etc. We overlook 'the lift' because as a society we have become inured to this 'overlook'. This mosaic of true stories challenges this conditioning and shows how not only despite the simplicity and banality of the everyday, but rather from it, happiness that belongs to an empowered space emerges – a happiness that is already extant and just awaiting our 'notice' of it and participation in it.

Each story in this book is moored in, and takes you through, different emotions that together celebrate life. *The Cherry Blossom Parting* celebrates poignancy and compassion; *Concealed and Packaged* traverses realisation and emancipation; *Relationships* negotiates the weight of hypocrisy; *The Vegetable Seller* cradles love and assaults inequalities; *I Miss Her* hypnotically reminds us to never take anything for granted, especially those we love while *The Nose Stone* is a searing comment on extant times where the intimacy and ordinariness of a nose stud is tied to the machinations of politics. One story told in poetry, *Draupadi and Me*, is historical yet a powerful comment on our times. Together, this tessellated companion is a minutiae of a journey to discover love, light, courage and hope and all that really matters to you *being you*. You can begin from any story in the collection – and read each story as independent of the others as each one has its own resonance.

Some of the stories have been experienced and written while I was living through my own disappointments in life and dealing with what we have been conditioned to perceive as loss. These stories 'happened' to me as I stayed open to the song of the universe through all times and gave a chance to the wonder of the smallest everyday things to unfold the greatest and sweetest joys. And then tasted the sweetness it added to life's journey. May each of you make this journey yours.

And as I just look out
The white butterfly
From my window
I hold in sight and in flight
A soul flight.
It flies with soul wings.

Ours alone

We are braver than we know
more tenacious than we are made to believe
many of us have returned from battles
without visible scars.
And many of us are in wars
we don't talk about
sifting through our fragments
that become mirrors.
All of us
are just so beautiful
through our caterpillar struggles
for they give us
the promise of flight
with butterfly wings.
And this knowing
is ours
and ours alone.

Colours in Us

London, Piccadilly Circus. The weather is deciding between whether to smile sun–like or frown grey cloud–like. Like typical British weather! But all of London and the world in London, is out to play.

Scottish bagpipers are playing by the Statue of the Horses of Helios. Just in front of the pedestrian circle a young man has a crowd gathered around him. He is trying to do Michael Jackson's Moonwalk. Among his audience is a pair of lovers, kissing with the familiarity of passion and the abandon of insecurity. A Spanish man tries to get his partner, a man in stilettoes, to do the salsa to the moonwalk music. Artists are sitting on the steps of Piccadilly's Circus. I can't see what they are drawing and painting but I wonder what stories their captures are telling.

I'm early for a meeting. I have about ten minutes to kill. So I let myself be serenaded by Piccadilly's 'Happy' Circus. The stories behind the smiles, is not what today is about. Just then I see a woman. Some women are stunning, gorgeous, glamorous. Some others attractive to the A. Some others still simply beautiful. This lady was simply beautiful, strikingly beautiful. A porcelain complexion, Princess Diana–esque coloured eyes. Her eyes were finding their way. And then they were still. She was blind.

I wanted to go and speak to her. I had to act in the flash of an eye or in that crowd she would have gone instantly. How do you approach a stranger on the road for no reason but their immediate beauty? And that too a stranger who can't see you back?

I went up to her and with her carer holding her elbow and watching, I said, 'I'm here for a meeting and I'm early. I just saw you and felt you are so beautiful that I wanted to come up and compliment you.'

She smiled looking ahead of me and chatted back for a few minutes. I told her about my upcoming meeting and she told me about how her boyfriend had organised a dinner date for her right up the road. And she came early 'to have some summer fun in the London sun!' Her face lit up when she spoke of her boyfriend. Of how he compensated for her lack of sight. Of how he helped her 'see' the world more fully and happily.

Our time was up quickly. She went her way. And I mine.

A friend I shared this experience with later said, 'Her boyfriend is not being realistic. How can he raise children with her, for example? Will she be able to dress them for school everyday? Do the school and activity rounds? Life is not a fantasy. It's about living in the real world,' he said. And I realised it was his conditioning speaking. He continued, 'It is unlikely that any eligible bachelor at least in our culture (referring to India) would take home a blind lady to his parents and introduce her as the lady he would like to marry, like to have children with. His family would think he has gone bonkers at best or they would be terrified that he might actually go ahead!'

The next day while speaking to another friend I brought up the topic of 'being realistic'. And I came up with this conclusion – yes there will be challenges to loving and being with a differently abled partner. But then don't even the best of relationships have their challenges? You could marry a perfectly abled partner and then s/he could develop issues. Or someone who has problems can become better or the problems subside with time. We all are human and intrinsically vulnerable. Anything can happen to anyone at anytime. Does that mean we stand disqualified to be loved? If being realistic involves ruthlessly qualifying and disqualifying people for love depending on how they are placed for a worldly existence, I'd rather leave realism along the way.

We all have colours in us. The same colours that I have, you have too. But yet we hide them from each other. Life is about connecting our colours such that we feel safe to reveal them. That then is a beautiful life. And what can possibly be more realistic than the experience of beauty during the gift of our human journeys?

Million Much

Early this morning on my way to a Brexit Conference my tube journey was interrupted. Interrupted by sweetness. At a station a little girl boarded with her mum and littler brother. She was probably about six years old and had Down's Syndrome. As she waited to get on the tube, holding her mum's hand, for every passenger that got off the train she said 'I love you!' I was struck that none of the commuters returned her loving gesture with a smile or an 'I love you too!' Perhaps the journey from sleep to full wakefulness, work, deadlines etc. didn't allow them the space to notice, to pause. What was even more striking, and beautifully so, was that her mum returned her every 'I love you' to the commuters with an 'I love you too!' When the little girl walked in to the train it was my turn. Her brother sat beside me, then the little girl and her mum, in that order. As she sat, she bent her head, looked at me and said, 'I love you'. And as the Paint Our World[2] children often say, I replied, 'I love you million much!' She beamed and got busy with her mum. I wondered if the beam was because I had responded to her gesture. And then after about two stops she reached her hand across her brother and tapped my coat. Her face smiled as she said, 'Million muchhh! I love you million muchh!' My unexpected gem of love first thing in the morning on a fast crowding London train! If only the other commuters had taken that pause too.

A Cherry Blossom Parting

It's Easter Monday. Still a holiday in London but I had writing deadlines so it was mostly a working day for me. I awoke at the crack of dawn to get to work. A magpie, like on most spring mornings in London, came to my window after sunrise to say hello. Today, I didn't make time to pause and respond to this bird of prettiness even though I noticed it came to my window many times more, than on usual days. Perhaps because, unlike other days, I did not go up to the window to say hello? I was writing furiously. But when I did take a pause from my writing for breakfast, the kitchen fridge told me that I had run out of milk.

It was a chilly morning. I hastily put on my coat, socks and shoes and I dashed to the corner shop to get some milk. On my way back I was stopped in my tracks. A magpie lay precariously between parked cars, its feathers splayed on the ground. It lay dead. As I bent down to see it, another magpie flew furiously around me and the beautiful bird, now lying motionless on the road. I asked myself – could this magpie, so agitatedly flying about, be the partner of the slain bird? Or perhaps a sibling? Or a best friend? Could this be the magpie that was at my window so many times this morning?

Were the multiple visits to my windowsill a cry for help? Or was it the now dead magpie that came visiting? Giving me a chance to say a 'goodbye hello'?

My mind grew numb. The birds, both the one lying lifeless and the other anxiously alive, felt like a stretched part of me. And my mind travelled back to my childhood.

I must have been all of three years old because this incident happened soon after I began school. It's funny how some childhood memories, even after all that passage of time, seem contiguous and take you back in time in such a way that it brings the memory into the present. I used to live in a multi–storeyed apartment block in downtown Kolkata. One afternoon, I returned from school to find a bird's egg tenderly broken and lying on my balcony floor. The eggshell was apart and a tiny bit of the foetus oozed out while the rest still lay precariously within the split shell. And a bird, perhaps the mother, sat by the broken egg. At times she would insanely fly the length of the balcony and then again sit by her egg. I was distraught. I woke my nanny up from her afternoon nap and summoned her help. I wanted to arrange a burial for the bird's baby lying dead in the broken egg.

My nanny thought I was insane but I persisted. That evening, like everyday, I did not go to play with my friends, because I was busy finding a burial ground for the bird foetus amidst teeming cars and car parks on Kolkata's congested downtown roads. I finally settled on a tree on the road which had some visible mud around it. I wet the mud with water from my school water bottle to make it easier to scoop out some earth which I did with the back of a pencil and I quietly laid the egg to rest. I remember feeling sad. And I think I was crying as I buried it.

After all these years, today, I recognised that three year old in me again. Even though, the two incidents seem separated not only by very different places but also seemingly different lifetimes! I brought lots of kitchen towel from my kitchen and then gently placed the magpie on it. Lifting it onto the kitchen towel brought back the same tears. I took it to the site of a cherry blossom in bloom nearby. A cherry blossom, the tree that symbolises beauty and the transience of beauty and life, could not have been more apt for this 'laying down'. I carefully laid down the magpie's electric blue, swan white, midnight black and emerald green little body. And I was not alone. The other magpie had flown with me. As I walked the tiny distance back home I wondered – will the magpie be back at my windowsill tomorrow morning?

The Prettiest Date

It was a balmy spring evening, quite uncharacteristic for London. On my way back from an event on politics, I stopped for dinner. I've been with myself for dates in London many a time. But somehow today, as the waiter ushered me to my table I felt a hint of loneliness. I wished there would somehow be someone on the opposite side of my table. Someone lovely and loving, someone to have a nice end–of–the–day conversation with. Someone I could learn from or love with.

My first urge as I sat waiting for my food to arrive was to take my phone out. But I resisted. T.S Eliot's words, and one of my favourite lines came to mind, 'At the still point, there the dance is.' And I stayed still with myself – a quiet, non–judgemental observer – even of myself.

Just then a little boy sitting on the table opposite me caught my eye. He was adorable and irresistibly cuddly and wore thick purple frames around his eyes. The glass frames, though perhaps the thickest I've ever seen on such a little boy, somehow added to his cuteness. And I felt we made eye contact – because we both smiled at each other at the same time. And rightaway, he left his seat and ran a tiny bit in the restaurant before going back to his seat.

My meal arrived and before I could put cutlery to my food I found this little being standing beside me saying, 'You are pretty'. His mum came right after him, reprimanding him, 'George, you don't disturb people when they are eating'. I told his mum he was just complimenting me and made me smile. His mum sounded a little surprised.

She said, 'He can't see very well at all so he can't really see you clearly. I'm surprised he has called you pretty.'

Standing just below my eye length as I was sitting, and reaching his standing mum's hips, he looked up at her and asked, 'Can we sit here Mummy?' pointing to the vacant space opposite me on my table.

Before his mum could reply I said, 'Please, I can't think of a better dinner companion than George!'

His mum remained hesitant, 'Are you sure? Are you expecting anyone? I don't want him to disturb your dinner.'

'He's not distributing,' I insisted. I convinced her and they sat opposite me.

We asked the waiter to get their food to my table. We chatted about our respective days, the menu, about London's beautiful springtime cherry blossoms and squirrels. I finished my meal first but enjoyed their company so much that I stayed on till they finished theirs.

Towards the end his mum was telling me about his condition, saying, 'I hope his eyesight does get better. He does not realise his eye sight is poor because this is his normal. He can hardly see properly.' And little George replied, 'I can Mummy. Preeya's pretty.' Now could I have asked for a prettier date? Life always has its ways to reach us with a smile!

The Real Magic

The British Museum, London. In the midst of a heaving crowd I'm gazing at the painting 'The Great Wave' by the Japanese artist Hokusai. Mesmerised by claws in the colours of teal, aquamarine and sky blue against a backdrop of cobalt. Hokusai's detailed brush strokes turn ocean waves into claws with Mount Fuji in miniature, at a distance. Then I turn to his other paintings like 'Important Places in China.' The attention to detail in his paintings is unfathomable. The detail just seems humanely impossible. A friend tells me Hokusai was autistic. 'He needed autism to get this level of mastery in detail.'

'His autism was then a gift here', I say.

'Yes, very autistic people can be hyper intelligent and insanely detailed. We are all arguably autistic – it's just about where on the spectrum of autism we are. Autism compensates in exceptional gifts for so many,' my friend explains.

And my mind recaps a recent conversation I had with a care worker who is caring for an autistic adult. This autistic man is Middle Eastern and lives in his parents' palatial home in one of the swankiest parts of London.

'His family come to visit him twice a year. Yesterday his sister came after half a year. In less than ten minutes my caree[3] held her hand and led her to the lift in the house. It was his way of saying he was not comfortable with her and did not want her there,' the special needs care worker tells me.

'Well his family are fortunate', I respond, 'that they can afford you and other care workers on shift like this'. I was told the caree has cleaners, cooks and care workers round the clock.

The care worker replies, 'No, not fortunate. In this case money, the excess of it, is a curse.'

He pauses. And continues. 'If they did not have so much money to leave him here in the hands of expert care and just pay him bi–annual visits, they would be here themselves. Or he would be in his country with them. He doesn't need me all night just watching over him if a family member can sleep with him. He does not really need the cleaner, the cook and all this expert help! He needs family. But he hardly recognises his family now.'

Being a special needs expert he explains more about autism to me. How the behaviours with this condition are tediously repetitive, how touch like hugs are shunned, how OCD (obsessive compulsive disorder) habits are an everyday reality yet they do respond to the familiarity of the presence and care of people.

And he goes on to narrate an experience from his family to elucidate how not to let 'excess' steal the little joys of life.

'Recently my daughter won a hamper at a fair. She loves chocolates and this hamper was gigantic, and in it was every possible chocolate that was a child's delight – Lindt, Cadbury, Kitkat, Tobler, Mars, Snickers and so many more. And oh boy did she love the sight of that hamper!'

'We went home. She took out all the chocolates and displayed them on the table. The table was crowded. They were just so many chocolates.'

'Two days later at the dinner table she surprised me. She said, "Daddy you can give all those chocolates away." I looked at her, totally puzzled. She looked back and said, "Daddy, I don't want so many, all together. I want to go with you every week to the supermarket and choose my chocolate for the week."

'That was what we usually do – a choice of chocolate is a staple of our weekly grocery shop. And I realised the real joy of life is not in getting it all, or too much and all at once. That's the problem with us now: some of us can get it all, or most of it, quite quickly. And then, yet, we find we can be awash with emptiness. The joy, the allure, is in the wait, in the work for what we want, so we cherish it.'

I think with it and concur – in the journey of working towards what we want, it is often in the experience of little things, where the real magic of life's journey lies. And along the way, whether autistic or not, each of us have our imperfections – and it is in our imperfections that our perfection often lies.

Just like Hokusai who wrote that he often lived in penury. And he religiously threw his daily paintings 'out of the window' because till he was fifty years old there were no takers of his work. Could he have known over a century later, halfway across the world, the British Museum – a Goliath of art, culture and history, would pay tribute to his work? People from across the world would come to applaud? That tickets for an exhibition of his 'unwanted' artwork would be almost impossible to get? And those with the chance to be awed by his work, would consider themselves the lucky ones? Hokusai, even in times of indigence, just kept doing what he knew best and loved most – painting.

A Lamborghini and an Old Lady

I saw a Lamborghini yesterday. It was parked right outside the Mayfair Hotel. London is aflood with Lamborghinis and especially in Mayfair and more so in summer. So what was special about this one? It wasn't the fact that it was stunning. Electric blue and black, it laid low and shouted out loud. There was an old lady standing right by it. She was beautiful. Wrinkled and with a scarf around her head she spoke in an Eastern European accent. She reminded me so much of Mother Teresa, even replete with the hunch and rubber slippers. She was struggling with the bags she was carrying. I asked if I could help her.

She gave me a kind smile and said, 'I just came to meet my son. He's visiting here' (and she pointed to the Mayfair Hotel).

Passers–by were delighting themselves with the sparkling car and she said, 'That's my son's new toy. He's done well for himself but I don't see him much anymore.' And as a young, in–love couple posed for a selfie with the car in the background, the old lady made her way to the tube station. To get home.

Make *Beleaf*

Lately, the sun has been at glorious play in London. In such weather, the outdoors beckon at every opportunity. So today, making the most of the sunshine, I took my lunch break in the park. As I took a breather after a rushed morning by sitting on a bench amidst sprawling greenery, taking it all in, a little girl came and stood by my bench. The bench was full of things people had left.

I asked her, 'Would you like to sit?' And she nodded endearingly. I bunched the stuff together to make place for her.

'What's your name?' I asked.

'Macken–zee', she said softly.

She looked at me toying with my phone in hand and said, 'Can we play make–beleaf?'

'Funny she's asking you', said her nanny who stood watching over Mackenzie's toddler brother who played in the patch of grass in front of us. 'Mackenzie's very shy, she doesn't easily talk to people and she wants to play with you! She's usually quite quiet. Aren't you Mackenzie?' she asked the little girl with a surprised smile.

Now my attention was off my phone and on Mackenzie's phone – a bubbly pink plastic with lots of pretty stickers and punch numbers. 'So in make–beleaf', and she took a deep breath, 'you call me and we can chat.' And I called her.

We chatted about our favourite colours, if the trees might be feeling hot too and what we like doing most in the park. She told me she was four and after her birthday she will be five and said she thought I was sixteen! After our chat my break time was up and as I rose to leave, she said, 'See, that's how you speak in make–beleaf. You can speak to anyone you want.'

Is that how you speak to your unrequited love? Or to someone you lost but want to find – perhaps your own lost self? Is that how I speak to my dad who is with his maker? In 'make–beleaf'?

I just wished to cuddle Mackenzie in a never–ending sort of way. An unexpected little playmate who taught me more than she could ever know. The smile from her eyes disappeared. She didn't want me to leave she said. She wanted to play – play some more make–beleaf.

Crevices

London, Hammersmith station. Rush hour. There's nothing unusual about the evening. The trains, as the 'overhead voice' confirms, are running on time: 'There is a good service on all underground lines'. The rush is palpable. There is a scarcity of time. Commuters are rushing through time to get home on a balmy summer evening. Some wear tired looks. Some wear the 'summer look'. But almost everyone is wearing the 'rushed look'. Except, I noticed, one little hunched lady. She was standing at the bottom of the stairs to the platform. She had a small petite frame and her face wore wrinkles such that I found the crevices of earth reflected on her face. As though the soul of the earth was conflating with the soul of her face saying, 'You are one with me'. We are always one with nature, we are born of nature and with age, this oneness becomes more visible. Her kind wrinkles reminded me so much of Mother Teresa. But this lady was crinkled and hunched – in a flood of tears. Amidst the non-stop frenzy, my 'notice' stayed on her and I asked myself if I should approach her or not.

My train stomped onto the platform but her kind expression made the decision for me. I went up to her and asked, 'Are you alright?' She looked up at me and said, 'No, I'm not.' She sobbed more before continuing. 'I lost my sister last week. And it's just so painful. She was my best friend for seventy–seven years. I just can't let her go.'

'I'm so sorry', I said and asked, 'Can I give you a hug to say I hope you feel better soon?'

She nodded quite vigorously for her feeble frame. I hugged her and on that super crowded station platform a little lady cried a little less. I led her to her train and then took mine on the opposite side of the platform. On the train I wondered, how many of us may not visibly be in tears at points in our life but might be crying within and hope someone would notice and reach out. When someone cares, reaches out and makes you feel better – that feeling pervades over the 'reality' of trying circumstances.

It also made me think yet again of the tragedy of separation from a loved one, not because of death, but because of life. When they can be 'reached' but can't be 'reached out to'. Because somewhere we let the rules, laws, and conditionings of life seep in. In Arundhati Roy's words, 'the rules that lay down who can be loved. And how. And how much.'

It is up to us, to pay homage to life. To rewrite these rules.

A Perfect Love in an Imperfect World

On a golden autumnal afternoon in London after a stroll in Kensington Palace Gardens I sat on one of the many benches surrounding the lake. The lake was bordered by trees in the process of letting go – in colours of sunset orange, turmeric, terracotta, copper and the prettiest hues of scarlet. An elderly couple sat beside me. The gentleman sat at the edge of the bench and beside him, in a wheelchair, his wife. The gentleman, Dave, looked upbeat complimenting the London autumn sun. The lady, his wife Haely, sat shrivelled. With her face buried in her left hand she sat frozen in that pose. Except for when she removed her hand to agitatedly rustle the nest of ash grey hair on her head. Around her there was beauty. White and blue took centre stage in two directions – the white clouds traversing the blue skies and the white swans, swimming in file, on the blue of the lake. A swan came before her and majestically spread its feathers. Again and again and again. A show so beautiful that it would put the faith of God in an atheist. A little girl watching, pranced and clapped in glee. She was smaller than the swan but her squeals of laughter occupied a much bigger, magical space.

Passers–by stopped, smiled at the little girl, watched the swan's display in awe and posed for photos. Except Haely, who showed no change in her facial expression. With her face still buried in her chin she simply moved her gaze downwards, staring at her socks and shoes that were done up like a schoolgirl.

She had Alzheimer's I learned. I struck up a conversation with her husband who began sharing as easily as only strangers can do – the easy sharing that comes when the fear of being judged does not creep in. He met Haely when he was a married man stuck in a failed marriage and had a clandestine affair with her.

'I gave Haely a very tough time', he said, 'I kept taking out the stress of my failed marriage on her. And she put up with me. She would always respond to my mean ways with compassion. But my behaviour often left her in tears and two years later, she left. She could no longer stay trapped, she told me. I didn't have the courage to tell my wife about Haely because I had three children under thirteen and my eldest son had Down's Syndrome. I feared if I was honest about Haely, my wife would leave taking the children with her. So I kept quiet and stayed duplicitous and trapped. After Haely I had fleeting affairs with other women too. I needed the distraction of affairs but no other woman put up with me or my situation for more than a few weeks. But then, in fact twenty–five years ago this month, tragedy struck. My eldest, whom I loved more than anyone, was taken away. His death was the last straw that officially broke my already broken marriage. My wife and I could not relate or even reach out to each other even though we were facing our biggest tragedy. Tragedy I was told brings people together, not with my marriage. I guess because the cracks were large and the light being let in through them just gave my wife and me the courage to break away so we could be the people we really wanted to be.'

'It was over a dinner of cod and chips two months after my son Joshua's death that my wife told me she had met someone and wanted out. I was fifty–two. I began my search for Haely. There was no social media and WhatsApp then. She had moved house and it took me few months to find her and then another two years to bring her back into my life. I proposed to her in the same coffee shop she broke up with me in. I used the space of a sad ending this time for a happy beginning. Haely and I got married and we had a good nineteen years together before she began her affair – with Alzheimer's. This time it's my turn to stand by her side. She does not really respond to anyone except me, and that too, only sometimes.'

Haely was still gazing at her schoolgirl shoes and socks.

More swans had sauntered into Haely's space and were busy with parading their antics. Haely continued gazing downwards. Just then Dave called her by her name and there was no response.

And then he said 'My Love' and she smiled. Dave looked at her and again said, 'My Love', and then at me, telling me, 'Now that's the smile I've always fallen in love with'. And Haely's face left her hand. She looked up at her husband. And smiled. Never before have I ever seen a more beautiful response to being called 'My Love'.

Maybe God Does Show Up?

Charing Cross Hospital, London. This hospital might be different in perception – that it is one of London's nicer hospitals. Being in the borough of Hammersmith and Fulham, one of London's nicest areas, it caters to the city's affluent people and that itself, arguably, is a qualification for being 'nicer'. It is plush, yes, in many ways. There are cafes and eateries, there is even a bookstore and a beauty parlour. But all that is before the 'patient area' begins. The area where suffering becomes another person – visible and egregious. Put your finger on the pulse of the hospital and it also feels just like any other. A place where humanity steps in. Where the care and love of those towards their loved ones' suffering becomes most palpable. And yet it is also a place where humanity steps out. When each patient becomes just that – a patient. It's all just clinical. People and their suffering converted into numbers. Numbers, to differentiate the pain of one from another's.

It's a place where humanity is defined in our shared vulnerability, in our common pain and it is a place where humanity is reconfigured in our fights with suffering.

While I waited in the waiting area, mobile hospital beds streamed in and out carrying patients for tests. The mundane hospital work of everyday. Except that the beds may have been inanimate but they carried people – real, alive and in pain. I saw a lady, not relatively young but not relatively old either – her face contorted in pain. Her eyes shut with pain. Her bed on wheels stopped beside me, waiting for the traffic of incoming beds to abate. She was wired up to machines that looked like suspended iPads. I lost count of the number of tubes put into her – her wrists, her nose, her mouth, her finger even. A speechless finger. She opened her eyes, barely, and I smiled at her. And her eyes opened a little more and lapsed back into shut. I couldn't even begin to fathom her pain. Was she a mother? I wondered. I felt like waving a magic wand to alleviate her pain and then I felt helpless in the face of her pain. And thought that if I – a stranger to her, could feel such helplessness at seeing her, I wonder what her family are going through?

Another lady in a hijab was tending to her disabled son on a wheelchair. Just stroking his hair. Putting his hands right only for them to keep turning inwards again. He had just had a seizure and had now lapsed into quiet, 'Till the next one,' his mother said. People came wearing neat crosses, the opaque hijab, and perhaps some wore their non–belief in a higher intelligence – differences that matter so much in our engineered world. But here, they had come just to seek remedy to their pain. They had all come from a separated world to a 'together' world. They were all in the same boat and had come to the same sea to seek the same lift of healing.

The slew of mobile beds moved and a vivacious care worker in blue brought a man on crutches to sit on a vacant chair beside me. She began asking him about his next of kin. He looked very young – perhaps twenty but said he was thirty–five. He insisted to her that he had no one – no next of kin to give. She pursued her asking – very kindly. He then elaborated that he lost his parents and has no friends here to mention. His wife he said, just disappeared. His daughter was killed by 'animals', before his eyes. He was a refugee from Syria. He knew war, he said, and surprisingly some Urdu. His care worker doubled up as an interpreter but he did not really need one, his conversational English was good but his accent brittle with pain.

He told me he had an accident. Then a surgery at Northwick Park Hospital in north–west London and now he had been sent here for further rehabilitation.

The care worker remained curious, even astonished, that this man had no next of kin.

He began telling us some of his story. 'This pain, this pain', he said, of the surgery, 'is nothing. For you it must be pain', he looked at his puzzled care worker 'because you don't know pain'.

'Have you seen war?' he asked us. Before we could respond, he said, 'War, once you have been in it, it does not leave you. It shows you, humans actually are brutes. I'm here but that war is in my head. The sound of gunfire, the fear, my daughter's blood – is still on my clothes, on my hands. The fear has gone. It has become pain. Her bullets are now in me'.

'Do you believe in God?' I asked.

'God? REALLY? God? Only people who have not seen real life, people like you, can believe in God.' He sounded exasperated with me.

'Can a God create such animals like humans? And if so, if he has created, I don't want to know him. He is just rubbish. All rubbish.' He spoke with helpless, bubbling anger.

'I just want this pain to go. It's there. ALL THE TIME. When I awoke from my surgery I was told I will feel no pain for a while. But I woke up to this pain. My life is hell. In my head. And God is shit, bullshit as you say in your English.'

Both the care worker and I tried to distract him with innocuous conversation, like – do we vote for tea over coffee and our thoughts of London snow! But he kept returning to the absence of God. His utter disgust of God and of 'his animals'.

I was called for my appointment. And I left quickly but wished him with a smile before I left.

After my appointment I saw he was still waiting in the waiting area. I went up to him and said, 'I hope you get well soon. And you overcome your pain. I have faith you can and you will heal.'

He looked up at me with an insouciant look that mellowed into interaction and said, 'You know, maaay–be you have a point.' And he repeated the words I had told him a short while ago. 'Maybe God does show up. Sometimes when you least expect. If not, why would a complete stranger like you come to wish me. And it feels like you really mean it.'

And he smiled at the nurse. She returned his smile with a burst of smiles and said, 'Now that's a first!'

When a Smile Is a Moment Away

A lady sitting near me on the tube today looked very sad. Her expression carried the weight of pain. No tears from her eyes but one could clearly see the tears 'in' her eyes. Opposite her, a little girl (all of five I guess) kept singing, 'Don't you wooorry about a thing, every litt–til thing is going to be o–right, so don't you wooorry...' She sang this tune non–stop in the most adorable voice and with the cutest accent. I slowly noticed the sad lady's expression ease, she slowly broke into a cautious smile to then begin smiling more spontaneously. It was as though that little girl had been sent just for her and with just the song she needed to hear. So never despair, even in your saddest moments, you never know – a smile might just be moments away.

When the Timing Is Right

It was a sun–drenched day. I was at my friend Siobhan's home in the British countryside. We had just returned from a long, meandering walk by a snaking river with blissful willows weeping into its muddy banks. We walked and talked – chatting about countries we had visited and lived in, parenting and just the loveliness of the day and savouring it together.

Back in her garden the smell of lavender was afloat. And every now and then it mingled with the sharp fresh fragrance of the rosemary bush just behind it.

We continued chatting over our warm salad lunch. The conversation turned to gardening and her children. Lunch over, I sat contemplating my journey home with some thought of awaiting deadlines. I was ready to check the train times back to London when Siobhan reappeared. This time with her laptop. Animatedly, she said, 'Come, come let me show you the prototypes I've been developing for my business'. I was engrossed. It was a brilliant idea spelt out here in a very captivating power point presentation backed by rigorous, unequivocally painstaking, research. She looked at me for my thoughts and just then her gaze casually returned to her notebook screen. And froze. Her fingers rose to her face – to complete the expression. She looked at me – her eyes tearing up. Then she looked back again at her screen.

It was the look I've seen on faces that has mapped itself on my memory in indelible ways. The look I saw as a child in a fellow child's eyes who was told his mother, who he watched being reduced by cancer, had finally beaten it. The face of a student being told her conditional application to Harvard, against the odds, has been accepted. The expression of a woman who was once crushingly told she would never be a mother, holding her new born. The look of a friend after her love, whom she was giving up on, proposed to her.

The expression of complete joyous disbelief.

Siobhan's tearing eyes turned to me, 'It's her. She has agreed! She will invest the entire amount. She is coming on board!' And in a voice of tears she read the email out to me.

It was an email from a potential investor, who for Siobhan's business idea was ideal in expertise, clout and wealth. This was the watershed moment that for fifteen years she had been hoping for yet not knowing if it would ever really arrive.

And then as she held my hand tightly and cried with joyous disbelief, she began recounting her entire fifteen year journey with her start–up proposition and all the vicissitudes that it came replete with. Lifting the veil shielding the story of sweat, tears, sacrifice, and relentless tedious work without tangible results, she acknowledged how none of this was possible without the unwavering support of her partner. She began alone and for fifteen years kept putting in her own money with no revenue output. She gave line–ups of presentations to investors, individuals and corporates only to receive nonchalant responses or condescending feedback. Yet she persevered. She had her 'times of doubt and exhaustion', which she overcame with conviction because this was an idea that she really believed in. A project she left her bill–paying job for. An idea that despite a sea of rejection she persevered with building and, over time, she pulled together a partner and put a team in place. But still the much needed investment and revenue churns were a far cry. Yet each year after year, day after day, she did not part with her belief in her idea.

As the poet Nick Laird says, 'Time is how you spend your love'. That's all Siobhan did. Spent her love on what she truly believed in.

How many of us give up because of the emotional and psychological fatigue caused by discouragement from people especially if it comes from those close to us, whom we hope would understand us? How many of us simply can't muster the courage it takes to leave a salary–paying job to pursue what we really want to do? Our contexts, our emotional and financial safety nets or not, do play a role in informing our choices. But often it is the fear of going against the crowd or of failure that stops us from being our authentic selves. And our authentic selves are our best selves. After all it is our journey and our choice whether we chose to live by a script written by others for us, or script the journey of our lives, ourselves.

The Enchanted Land[4]

It's straight out of a fairy tale – this island. Every step taken on the cobbled roads holds a surprise. There are stone arches that seem to appear and disappear and there are parks that suddenly surprise you with sea birds and sky birds grazing, and bursts of flowers that hide behind lush greenery appear without notice. Multicoloured houses in ochre, yellow and pink appear to have been brought to life straight from a child's colouring book. And then the windows – stone windows right around the circumference of the island take you to beautiful views of the sea. From the windows in the distance you can see the land of the nearest city. Every fifteen to twenty minutes I would see a person. One could clearly tell if they were an inhabitant or a tourist. The inhabitants had a demeanour of hobbits – just at ease and happily going about their day. Cycling, walking their dogs, the children playing unsupervised by any adult. A 'hobbit' inhabitant tells me, 'This is a very special place. I was not born here but chose to come and live here six years ago'. Another shares, 'Thank God, unlike in cities our children here can roam and play completely unsupervised'. I saw children as little as six walking alone to their friends' houses to play. Even when it rained it felt like an enchanted rain from enchanted skies. I felt like Alice in Wonderland more than I did when reading the book of that name as a child. The feeling of enchantment swept into me and I became an enchanted adult. Just then a child of tourist parents said to his parents while he tried to climb up and over a raised cobbled fence, 'I love this place. I want to stay here'.

'This is not a place to live', said his mother. 'It is only a place to visit.'

And the child frowned and asked, 'But why? 'No I also want to live here. And play here', he insisted, looking at hobbit children somersaulting on wet grass. And frowned to the ground.

'Come on, walk straight,' was the response he got.

Why do we create a life where wonder and enchantment are not a place to live but only to 'visit'? And then we wonder how we are doing everything right and yet getting it wrong.

The Story Her Eyes Carried

Winter had just begun its ascent into Delhi. Climbing on to the pleasant evening air. And on to friends gathering for more outdoor meets after the slumber of the intense Delhi summer.

I had just landed into Delhi from London and was meeting my friend Danny – a footballer from north–east India. After an intense and very rewarding day with the children at Paint Our World, Delhi we met at a newly opened cafe. It was sedate with an air of classical music. I was on a Paint Our World high (overjoyed to see the children after a spell of a few months). We were talking all things Paint Our World. A friend of Danny's had also joined us, so the conversation turned to her as well and to telling her about the children's charity. She was intrigued and all ears. Just then an elderly couple sitting nearby interrupted, asking for a picture with Danny. With a shy smile, he obliged.

Just as he returned and we returned to more general chatter, a young lady came to our table.

She was dressed very smartly. But her crisp attire was not the striking part as compared to the story her eyes carried. She was the manager of the cafe. She looked at Danny with a 'dream come alive look' in her eyes and said, 'I'm so happy to have you in our cafe today. I'm from the north–east too and I've played football and you made that happen. You've been my inspiration all along.'

I've often heard from Danny the myriad challenges he faced in his journey from a little village in the north–east, to becoming a successful Indian footballer. The selfie seekers all see the gloss of his story, very few understand the courage of his story, the loneliness at times, and the constancy of commitment his journey required from him. Somehow, I felt this young lady's eyes said – she understood her hero's story. She told us she played excellent football and ran a football fraternity. With football dreams in her eyes she was now a cafe manager. Her passion for football though was still unequivocally palpable.

In India, talent at the grassroots level, especially in football is rarely spotted and developed. In the case of a female football player, it's unheard of.

This lady had met Danny for the very first time. So he essentially was a stranger, but his story was familiar to her. Not only familiar but also empowering. It probably gave flesh and blood to the barebones of her dreams. I felt she was more 'joy–eyed' than starry–eyed speaking to Danny. For her, he was symbolic of her football journey, albeit while he saw his passion through, she had to give hers up in the quest for a 'cafe–life'.

What motivates each of us is not really the 'person' of our heros and heroines (whom we mostly don't know personally) but their stories. It is the meaning that we give their story that empowers our own journeys. To give flight to our hero/heroine within.

And as I have learned and keep reiterating to the Paint Our World children and to myself in my 'self talk' the hero is formed not in the destination, but in the everydayness of the journey.

The cafe manager insisted on not letting us get the bill, telling Danny, 'For all you have done to inspire me, the least I can do is get you coffee'.

I replied, 'But I must pay because I don't even understand football! But seeing you, I will make an effort!' And her eyes smiled – the smile that carried the dream of many years.

Concealed and Packaged

Lunchtime in London. A buzzing organic cafe. I'm with a friend. We get our salad plates and juices and sit down to eat, drink and chat.

She's wearing a brightly coloured sari with a print that brings the likes of figurines on Indian temple carvings alive. Her hair cascades around her shoulders and she hugs herself saying 'I've been having a spell of low blood pressure for a week now. It makes me feel colder than usual'.

'Why didn't you carry something warm?' I ask.

'With a sari?'

'Yes, a shawl'. I answer.

'But it was so warm in the morning, who would know it will get nippy?'

'London's mercurial moods!' I remark and we laugh together. If anyone wants to know what mood swings are, you've got to live in London! The weather will give you ample practice at dealing with them!

'Did you have low blood pressure on Sunday too?' I ask her.

I attended her dance performance in London that Sunday called 'Burnt'. A powerful, unsettling performance in the Indian classical dance form of Kuchipudi, that told the story of Sati, the now outlawed practice where women were forced to immolate themselves on the funeral pyres of their husbands in India. The women were often child brides.

The logic: a woman being her husband's asset, must go up in flames with him. Without him she has no purpose, she becomes a liability on society. Her husband, in his manhood, would earn his place for his corpse to be burnt. For the woman, his widow, she earned herself no such honour, no such civility that waited for natural causes to lay claim to her mortality. Her ear splitting shrieks would be doused by 'a–live' flames. That would scorch her from being a liability to those who laid down the rules. For generations. Of which gender could live, how and for how long. And how they must die. Or be burnt a–live. For love, is what they said – woman to her man.

Cases of Sati have been reported in India even in the twenty–first century.

Punctuating the gathering cafe chatter, my eyes travel to Arunima and I exclaim in amazement, 'You managed that intense, high–octane performance with low BP? It's gotta be the love of dance and your connect with the subject of Sati that powered you?'

'Totally', her eyes brighten and travel, stopping to speak with sadness and resolve, with vulnerability and defiance.

'If it made you uncomfortable just to watch my piece just try and imagine what it must be like for the women who were immolated?' And it continues, this Sati–state. As women, we all are perpetually sacrificing ourselves. Our sacrificing has become a naturalised state to be in. We are always putting others before us, while we keep falling behind! And the trick within us is, that we don't even realise, it's so normalised.

As women, we have travelled from being fed to the flames (in India), to feeding our desires, our honesty, our authenticity, our dreams – to the flames, little by little. A lift of flame we keep allowing in, to engulf that little bit of us – that tiny part of our heart, that spot of soul.

During a recent discussion on a table of 'intellectuals' a high–powered, married couple's promiscuity was mentioned. The woman was called 'a keep to many'. While the man who shared his wife's promiscuous reputation, was spared any such nomenclature. I was aghast!

A slut, a whore, a prostitute, a call–girl, a mistress – all belong entirely to a woman, ascribed especially for her tenor, the same tenor that celebrates her for giving life and nurturing it. Men are normally above such sobriquets!

A woman really ought to be lauded, just for being her, a person, just as a man is. We are made differently, we think differently, and so we are made to work in tandem but not in hierarchy. Our differences are what create the need for us to couple, we are complementary yet deserving the same dignity. Being different means just that, it does not mean we stand disqualified from being seen with equal dignity.

Arunima's performance did not just look at history. It was extremely unsettling because it brought home the 'immolations' of women that continue to this day. Sati is not a one time immolation. It's the little immolations – everyday – unheard, unvoiced, quiet, subdued and engulfed where the injustice of it continues – just this time, twenty–first century style, it's neatly concealed and packaged.

Acid

When I boarded a plane recently little did I realise that an ordinary domestic flight in India would become an extraordinary experience.

I boarded the plane most ordinarily and took my seat. I was in the middle of making a last minute call when a lady tapped me on my shoulder. I was struck by the shine in her eyes and smile. 'That's my seat', she said, pointing to the vacant seat beside mine.

I came out of my seat to make way for her. She had long dark hair which she kept in place with a simple, functional, black hair band. She was wearing a red *salwaar kameez* that carried the heaviness of Indian marital attire. Based on her get up she could have passed as a new bride.

People passing our row on the aisle, who noticed her, almost paused; a few hurried their gait. Their expressions were confused, a caught confusion like when one is unexpectedly confronted with something uncomfortable and in that instant simply does not know where to look.

Somewhere, somehow we began an easy conversation. I tell her I live in London and travel to India to work with children.

'Are you married?' she asks.

'Yes', I reply. 'Married to positivity!'

'I'm seriously asking'.

'Nope! I'm single.' I seriously answer.

'Be wary of Indian men,' she warns me with a palpable anger. An anger that you could almost touch. And feel.

I know where she is coming from, what she is about to share. I'm intrigued but mostly aghast as she begins her story.

'You have kind eyes. The sort that put people at ease. Somehow I'm at ease talking to you even though we've just met. I was seeing a man,' she tells me.

'A man I loved even more than my parents or so I felt. I was with him for three years. We had made plans to introduce each other to our families and to get married. For three years we had kept our relationship secret. I did this on his insistence. Only he would often ask me not to call and message him. He would at times meet me at an interval of three to four months. He said his mother had cancer and he needed to be with her. He did not want to tell her about me as I was from another community and caste and he did not want to add to her distress in any way. I tried to understand and support his thinking at every turn. But throughout I felt uneasy. I had my doubts. But not the courage to voice those doubts to him assertively. I would bring it up often but meekly and he would get defensive, then offensive.'

'One day, on an uneventful morning I got a nasty message, followed by a call from an unknown number. It was a screaming and swearing woman – the wife of the man I was going to marry! Yes, that's how I learnt he was married. Separated but still married and now the woman wanted him back.'

'What happened after that was devastating for me. It was horrible. He tried to defend his lies when we met. I called him a fraud and a bastard and when he tried to force himself on me I slapped him harder than I thought I could.'

'The rest is history. He sent someone to throw acid on my face. I wear the pain of my heart, my foolishness in love – on my face, for all to see.'

Tears slid from her eyes into the black crinkles on her face. Raw pink bits made crevices between the crinkles. Where sadness lodged. Where anger took hold. Where resoluteness was taking shape.

I could sense my anger simmer – anger that such crimes are still abounding with impunity. Such savagery we are capable of and we call ourselves the 'human' race?

Seated in our seats with seatbelts fastened I gave her a half hug and told her, 'You are beautiful – in your smile, in your fortitude, in your resoluteness. And in the courage you thought you never had.'

She said, 'I don't even know you yet I know I will never forget how you just made me feel'.

Maya Angelou's words came to mind and I shared them with her: People may forget what you say or do but what stays is how you made them feel.

Festive Dinner

Away from the festive notice and cheer, the lights and dazzle, I was at a quieter Christmas dinner. A lady sat beside me. The pretty little white embroidered flowers on her black shawl offset the pain that was holding on to her eyes.

Her smile wrote the alphabets of a resigned sadness. Of those times when a smile becomes just the perfect cover for a 'life in stifle'.

We were social acquaintances and this time we began chatting. She had just been blessed with a grandchild and I congratulated her.

That led to an easy conversation. At first.

'The baby keeps me busy. I'm so busy seeing to her things. I don't know where but the whole day just goes. Last year when I lost my husband I felt a little lost but now with the baby I have someone to look after again'.

People sauntered past with plates full of food and faces full of pleasantries waiting to be exchanged. Some of them who knew either me or Anu stopped by to exchange greetings. Barring these banal punctuations, Anu continued pretty much unabated about her story.

She recounted how she got married very young when she was barely out of college, 'a bride with stars in my eyes'.

'But marital life was not what I expected. My husband was nice but my in–laws were very demanding. Then my son was born. I was handling him and home and my in–laws' demands. They would not get out of bed till I myself would serve them their breakfast, in bed for my mother–in–law, on the table for my father–in–law.'

Then she paused. The pause that fills life up with everything but your little desires; but your script for yourself.

'When my son became a teenager, my father–in–law had a stroke and became paralysed. And my mother–in–law became a heart patient.'

In between, she took pauses to take in the views of passers–by and to 'gulp out' a narrative, that twisted a life script, in a banal, matter of fact way.

'My father–in–law became frustrated. For four years he was on the bed. He would abuse my mother–in–law. When she stayed away being a heart patient, the abuses then naturally fell on me.'

What makes frustration so helpless that we unleash it only on those who don't have much choice but to tolerate it, on our closest and most loved ones? What is frustration's proximity to love? I wondered.

Anu continued, 'Then my father–in–law passed away and my mother–in–law became of all him and more. Frustrated, cruel and manipulative.'

She cited heart wrenching examples of utterly unnecessary cruelty. Cruelty in the little everyday things that can twist a smile into suffering.

'What was your husband's response?' I asked.

She smiled a careful smile.

'He was a very mild soul. Very kind to even a stranger so never said anything to me or to his parents.'

Is mild a euphemism for spineless? I wondered.

'My mother–in–law passed away, my son was still in University. I finally felt now my husband and I will have some time to ourselves. Now we had a chance at life.'

All the while, in between talking, Anu kept smiling out of sadness.

'But life had other plans. In three months he was diagnosed with diabetes and hypertension. In no time he had his first heart attack. Then the kidney failure began and then the second heart attack that took him away.'

Her sad smile continued but I felt tears well in my eyes. Why did she wait for life to give her a chance? Is life not about making our chance 'within it'?

Without any ponder, Anu continued.

'Now it's my grand–daughter's time.'

I said something totally unrelated. I looked at my plate and said the *gajar ka halwa*[5] looks nice. It was my way to cope. And I saw her plate – her spoon fiddling with the winter dessert. And she looked to me and said, 'Atleast he [her husband] saw our son's marriage'.

A few chair rows away her daughter–in–law was waiting for her to finish her dessert and take over the baby.

Santa Does Exist, After All!

Just when the festive feeling was gathering pace, a chance encounter led to an intense experience. A young lady began telling me about her experience of heartbreak.

'This fun and frolic makes no sense to me, I feel barren. Just heartbroken. I'm feeling anything but Christmassy.'

The man she loved and believed was the one for her had let her know he was now with someone else. That actually he had been with someone else for sometime. All the while trying to placate her doubts with the assurance that she was the one for him. Now he was seeing a girl whom his family thought was more appropriate, is what he told her. She was from a 'better' family, he said. (Just to clarify 'better' did not connote a family tenor–ed by goodness. It meant a family with a fatter bank balance.) So his alliance with this new lady, he believed, will make his family happier.

The logistics of marriage. And especially Indian marriages can take on a ruthless practicality. Or is it singularly telling about the guy to be dating a woman for a significant period of time to then unceremoniously tell her that she can't give his family the happiness another woman can, premised on her father's bank balance.

She struggled and spoke to me choking, 'All the times we shared, does it mean nothing? The reel of memories is playing in my head like a broken record. It's torturing me. And yet all I want to do is run to him.'

As I listen to her, I wonder what is it about us, about human nature that we care and care so profusely about those who treat us with such disdain. Who let us know we just don't count.

I wanted to tell her about the importance of self–care and self–love especially at a time like this. But she was so distraught that I wondered if anything I said will be received.

So I just looked at her light eyes and said, 'You have beautiful eyes'.

'It's been a while since anyone paid me a compliment.' She replied.

She tells me about a person we both know who told her that I tend to see the positive in life. 'Now I know what she means', she exclaimed.

'Well you are pained yes, but your eyes are still very beautiful. It's just a fact.' I was hoping she would smile.

But instead she just burst into tears. I reached for her hand and she hugged me. I hugged her back and held her while she cried. When she stopped she looked at me and said, 'I had always imagined him holding me if I needed to cry. But today it is not him but you who is comforting me.'

I replied, 'The universe does not always send us the person we ask for. But it does send help, even if it is in the form of another person.'

Santa does exist, after all. He just comes to us incognito. If only we believe. The universe does have our back. So the universe sends us Santa–like fronts! Especially during trying times. If only we keep the faith.

A Dip in the Ganga

India had just celebrated the festival of Makar Sankranti. This festival marks the day when the sun begins its ascendancy into the Northern Hemisphere.

In some apartment block rooftops in Mumbai, children were flying kites. Sending them into the winter sun, the skies receiving them playfully. For the adults, and some children too, taking selfies had replaced the kite flying. The significance of the kite flying was sadly unbeknown to all – the adults and the children. The kites here signify God's guidance to go higher and higher. In other words, away from darkness and into the light. But rituals, without an understanding of their purpose, is religion hollowed out, philosophy usurped, spirituality lost.

At such a celebration I began a light–hearted conversation with a domestic worker. She was dressed in a sari bedecked with turmeric and cherry red flowers. The colours were a loud compliment to her petite frame.

She happily confessed, 'I took a holiday today. I didn't go to work anywhere. My mistresses were cribbing but who cares?

What are festivals for, if not for taking holidays?' and she smiled with an enacted nonchalance.

'So did you go and take a dip in the Ganges?' Taking a dip in this river, holy to the Hindus is known to absolve one of one's sins and this is a popular time for bathing in the River Ganga.

'That's for the sinners, not me!' she chuckled.

'But aren't we all sinners, in some way or the other?' I asked her casually.

'You might be, I'm not!' came a defiant answer.

'Actually my husband could be, certainly not me.'

'Your husband?' I asked.

'Because he beats me black and blue.'

A momentary silence descended and she looked up at the skies – the kites gave respite to her thoughts.

As children squealed, her travelling eyes stopped on me and she said, 'He hits me because I deserve it. Sometimes when I don't listen and I rebel. Or don't let him do what he wants to do. Or fight for our children to continue to go to school.'

I was not surprised but yet I was aghast and I felt anger brewing in me. It is not uncommon for wives and especially for the demography of domestic helper wives to experience such violence at the hands of their husbands.

'And you tolerate it? You earn enough to move out and support yourself and your children alone.' I said.

'Yes, yes he pays nothing. Infact he takes from me for all his bad habits. But now he is ok. He does not beat me regularly anymore. He's reformed. Beatings are now just once or twice a month. And that's fine.'

'That's fine?' I was shocked at how she was normalising the violence perpetuated at her, more so regular violence.

'If I don't listen and I act smart of course he will hit me because I am the one provoking him. If a woman will not listen to her husband, the husband is bound to hit her. And each man has his vices. Every man has atleast one. Be it gambling, prostitution, alcohol. Now if I stop him, he will get upset and then he raises his hands on me. Kicks me even, if I answer back.'

The power of conditioning hits me. How in the twenty first century, in a fast developing nation, a gender can be made to believe that it is their role to be subaltern. That subservience is their DNA. That their inferiority to man is a daily reality that gives a man the right to his ways over a woman, even if that means using violence to achieve his dominance.

'It is not OK for an adult to hit another. It is clearly not ok for your husband to hit you on the smallest of pretexts. Nothing will change for the better if you accept this as OK, as normal.'

'And what do I do? Not accept the truth about the place of a woman with a man? Be a rebel? I have no interest to be a single woman like you! Single women have no respect. Atleast as a married woman I have the respect of my relatives and my community.' Her voice was raised and she was literally fighting back at any rationale I was trying to give her that her husband was in the wrong and she had a duty to stand up for herself. Not seeing much point in trying to reason with her I became quiet. After all, she was on holi–day.

She interrupted my silence with a playful chuckle in her eyes, 'I should teach my husband a lesson after all. I should have an affair. That will serve him right. But then if he found out, then he would chop me into pieces and throw me into the Ganga. That's how I will reach the Ganga', she laughed. A frightened and rebellious laugh.

She then sat down squatting, her hands resting on her knees and reaching beyond them. Her eyes travelled upwards and with them the big flowers on her sari – all looked heaven–ward – to trace the path of the criss–crossing kites.

Then, all of a sudden, she stood up and smiled. Slyly. Of a bare victory. And called out to me, as I was about to leave.

'What the heck, you know I will. I will have an affair. And this can be my dip in the Ganga!'

Valentine's Day!

On New Year's Eve, just after I had returned from a very moving day spent with specially abled children at Mother Teresa's Kolkata orphanage, I received a message. It was from a very dear friend in London. It was a light–hearted forward. A light heartedness that came bundled with poignancy. It said, 'Don't worry you are single today (31st Dec!). Valentine's Day is 44 days away and you will be single then too!'

Like me, my friend was over thirty and single! Single! A dreaded, reverberating word especially if you are post thirty, a woman and more so, if you are in India! Forget the fact you may be married to life, to your work, or to whatever gets you out of bed, with a smile, in the morning. Unless, you are married. To a man. It does not really count, does it?

Never mind if the man might be someone you've settled for and not one you genuinely connect with. Or one who does not value you. That's for another time.

Today it's about the approach to Valentine's Day. A dear friend in Delhi, knowing I will be in the city around that time urges me to stay back. 'Spend Valentine's evening with me', she said. 'Come home. We will have a nice evening at home.'

'But your husband will throw me in the Yamuna!' I replied. 'He will say, you may be single, but I'm not!' And we both laughed together, like old friends do.

'Priya, you will love his company and he yours. Be with us for Valentine's evening.' She insisted lovingly.

And our conversation turned to the 'fuss' of V Day.

When you love someone, Valentine's Day is everyday we agreed. And she said gently, 'Let me give you an example from this morning. I had a long day ahead and maybe it was the anticipation of all the work awaiting me, I'm not sure but I didn't sleep too well. At 5am, half asleep, I was saying, "Water". My husband who knows I drink only warm water, especially in winter, heard me and woke up. He went to the kitchen, put the kettle on and got me some warm water. His care is of the everyday,' she tells me. And my heart smiled to hear that. And I told her, 'That's love, the small everyday things. Which you deserve so much, which every woman deserves from her man, and every man from his woman. And love, which we get from not just our partners'.

Love, which we get in myriad ways. I think of all the ways love reaches me. All the ways it has found its way to me, and a place in me, most recently. When a friend gave me well meaning feedback because she cares; when friends came together to mark my Birthday in advance because I won't be in town on the day; when a friend gifted me a card she said was 'heart written'; the gift of a sheer cashmere scarf from a friend with the thoughtfulness that I keep warm on my frequent stays in colder climes; the joy in a Paint Our World child's eyes as she teaches me to draw; a friend marking her child's Birthday with me. I hear you say it is not enough. And it not the same. As a man's love. Yes, it is not the same. Unequivocally. And a single person will tell you that just as vehemently as a partnered person. The chemistry of the opposite sexes it does elide. Love, nevertheless, it still is. And does everyone who has the chemistry, have the love?

A man who will be love may arrive. Or he may not. The key is for each of us to live with love. Because it is the purest and highest emotion a human being can experience in this journey called life. And not because we are in anticipation that a romantic partner will arrive.

Here's to LOVE! And not just on Valentine's Day.

Relationships

I'm in a doctor's clinic in Kolkata. A fairly young foreign lady was sharing the paling sofa with me. We were the only ones there. We had both arrived early. 'Even the doctor *sahib* has not come yet', we were told. Amidst the dust green walls and aproned staff, we sat waiting.

A receptionist was getting irritable on the phone. 'Aajke hoaw–be na' (Today is not possible), she said peremptorily in Bengali. A calendar presided over her with a beautiful image of Pangong Lake in Ladakh. The lake sat serene in its make–up and still on the calendar wall. Except for the occasional dance of the page whenever the clinic door was opened and closed.

'Are Indian hospitals always so noisy?' the lady asked me. Her sharply angled cheekbones narrowing her hazel eyes into a smile.

'Here? Yes, pretty much', I replied.

'Where are you from?' I asked.

'Paaree', she answered in a heavy French accent.

'Nice! What brings you to India?'

'Well, my best friend. But he is no longer my best friend,' she said with the honesty sometimes possible only when the weight of judgement lifts – when you are complete strangers to each other.

Her hazel eyes travelled, to a place of loss. Her smile became loss shaped too.

'I'm sorry. Was he Indian? If it's ok to ask about him?'

'He's Mee–wari.' she answered replete with her French accent.

'Marwari?'

'Yes.'

'Wow! You know the denominations.' I was impressed.

She laughed. 'I didn't know or cared when I met him in Parree. But here I realise all this becomes important. Being Indian is not ei–nouff, no?' She asked with a profound simplicity.

And we began speaking about boundaries. Of race, nationality, and the 'within nationality' boundaries. And our conversation meandered into one about gender. There is a charm in meeting someone and plunging into a conversation of meaning and ideas even before you've introduced yourselves conventionally to each other. The ideas become a new form of introduction. The meaning in the conversation has a power of connectivity all of its own.

I began telling her that I was doing a series of talks on gender and #letstalkchange in India. And her eyes suddenly regained the look of loss and she asked.

'Can I ask you about Indian marriages?' and her far–away look of loss became present.

'Indian marriages!' I exclaimed.

'Sure you can but before you do just know you are speaking to a single person who has never been married and who has lived abroad for the best part of her life!'

'Yez, but still... you know, you must know more than me.'

'You know this perception, that marriage is India is zo strong and great. Really? Iz it really like that? Zoo goood? Zoo strong? From wiz–in?'

And she led me into the story of the best friend she lost, without understanding how come.

They met in Paris at a Michael Jackson dance class. Where she did the moonwalk better than him! She was a design student, he was studying business at INSEAD. He stayed back to get some work experience before he joined his family business back in India. 'H–and that's when we became real goood friendzh. I had a boyfriend then so for me it was clearly just friendship but Sayanz may have liked me, I don't know. I just know he was kind, and we got on zuu–perr well and did things together. H–and we shared verrymuuch.'

'Then I came to India with my friends h–and he joined us. We travelled together – Goa, Kerela and Myzore. When he came to France we did the French Alps togezer. But this time I've come to India he iz married and changed compleeetlly. He refused to invite me home but was happy to meet me zecretly outside. He asked me not to call unless he does. I could not understand it. He said h–is wife does not like me when she has not even met me once! How could she decide? How possibly? Tell me?' The exasperation in her voice, and the let down, were both palpable.

'The final thing was just zo weird. I just sent him a forward on whathsapp. Just a forward, nothing perzonal. The next morning he called me and got zo h-angry for sending a whatshapp at night. I could not imagine him being zo rude. I got upset. In France you can't treat a friend like thiz. There was no reason for such crazy nonsense and I said to him then that I can't be friendz like this and not to call me again.' A tear of incomprehension slid down a cheek.

'And tzat was it. Really. A friendship, a best friendship of years finished.'

Sadly, this was not the first time I was hearing about friendships between different genders ending because of an over possessive partner.

I recalled some of my friends here, beautiful people in themselves, yet telling me they keep checking their husbands' phones. And men here telling me their phones are checked regularly. Is a forced control better for the happiness of any adult, married or not? Clasping sand tightly in one's palms – will that mean the sand will stay more tightly or slip away more easily?

Is the longevity of a marriage or any human bond, at the cost of happiness, at the cost of lives skewed, a matter of pride? Is it a matter to hold your head high for the great and the long? Especially when controls really mean the trust has quietly slipped away, that it has slid into doubt. That familiarity has slid into strangeness. Between two people such that the control begins imposing a strangeness onto other friendships too. It begins imposing clipped wings. When life is about spanning wings. For ourselves and others. Here's to 'spanned winged' individuals. And marriages. And friendships. Even between different genders because aren't we people, first and foremost? Here's to 'winged relationships' before the 'great' and the 'long'!

Draupadi and Me

Lord Krishna is the most popular Hindu God. He is worshipped for His teachings in the Hindu holy book, the Gita. He is celebrated in His birth anniversary each year, with the festival of Janmashtami. He is revered for His role in the Mahabharata (the Great War) – the Indian epic that is the longest epic in the world. The Mahabharata is a metaphor for the Great War between good and evil within each of us that surfaces multiple times in each of the decisions we make, in the paths we choose. If there is any text in the world that can rival Shakespeare's work as far as an insight into human psychology goes, it is the Mahabharata where Lord Krishna plays a central role. However, one of Krishna's most central roles is that of his connect with Draupadi, a Princess who in the Mahabharat marries five Princes – the Pandav brothers who are the central characters of the epic. It is Draupadi's public disrobing by her extended in–laws that makes certain the approach of the Great War or the Mahabharata between the cousins – the Pandavas and the Kauravas. I've written this poem in Krishna's voice, where He laments, that in our increasing mistreatment of women and the trivialising of a friendship between a man and a woman who are not related by blood or by marriage, we have forgotten and elided the sacred element to a man–woman

66

bond. And He recounts the sacredness and meaning of His bond
with Draupadi and urges us to follow his example. If only each
of us can bring this awareness to our conditioning and then to
our everyday interactions with the opposite sex in general, the
possibility of such bonds are born.

You know me best in the words I spoke to Arjuna
on dharma and karma
on life and death
on all that lies thereafter
and in between.
You visualise me most in my supreme form
of Lord of heaven and earth and fire and sea and space
that I showed Duryodhana in his father King Dhritarashtra's
court
when I went as a messenger of the Pandavas with a peace
proposal
and the arrogant Duryodhana tried to imprison me.
The form I revealed to Arjuna, the greatest warrior of his
time, on the battlefield of Kurukshetra
when Arjuna was unable to lift his weapons to fight parts of
his own blood family.
But do you ever remember me for my bond with Draupadi?
who you know better as the one wife of the five Pandav
brothers
and the one who was publically disrobed in the presence of
her mighty husbands
by members of their extended family
till I came to her rescue.
But did you ever understand our bond –
Draupadi's and mine?
We were not related by blood yet
our bond was more sacred

than any blood relation could prove.
I was her friend
her confidant.
I saw trust, faith and surrender in faith
in her
her faith in my irrefutable presence in her path, in her joys
and her turbulence.
To me she was respect in every form.
Even I surrender to Shakti.
But you?
You follow my story.
You read my teachings in the Gita.
You worship me in temples.
But you have forgotten
how to recognise Shakti
to know her
to respect her.
Even when she is not your blood family.
I lament this you have forgotten
no remembrance of me is complete without the story of
Draupadi and me.

And I Miss Her

This morning, a crisp January morning was unfurled by meaningful conversation. I was drawn into a chat with some of my close friends on behaviour styles – aggressive, passive, assertive and passive aggressive. We honestly and authentically shared about our styles, our learnings and our will to transform to a place of more self–love and awareness and so we can give and receive the nurture required for more fulfilling relationships with ourselves and then others.

We discussed the roadblocks to creating healthy and loving bonds. When a loving connect disintegrates into a difficult one, what should we do? Should we keep giving our love and understanding even though we are also hurting and the other person seems unwilling to receive or reciprocate our work on the relationship? A point was discussed that if someone we value is not responding to our overtures is it best to exercise acceptance and patience, i.e., wait with the love we have for them in our hearts, for their revert? Just then a tragic story came to mind. One of learning that we don't really have the luxury of the 'the wait'. It is a luxury that risks the human experience of love with it. If only, both people in any human bond understood this.

A couple of years ago a gentleman spoke aloud to himself while speaking to me. He shared part of his story with me – of a woman he lost – to then love *in* loss.

He first met her at a University event.

'I can never forget how she was both intelligent and attractive. Not a conventional looker, but there was something very striking about her. Later I found her caring too. Caring to a fault. You know that rare combination that you get in chick flicks maybe?'

His suit looked crisp and unaffected by his speak and, quietly and starkly, began mismatching his expression.

'I still remember even though it was all those years ago. The white and black top that she wore over black jeans and with black boots. Simple and svelte. I was instantly attracted to her. Later at a conference I heard her speak and take questions. That's when I realised she was brains too.'

He fidgeted with the coffee cup in his hands. From one hand to the other. Like the effort of trying to get somewhere when you are stuck.

'That day I took her number, called her, courted her a bit. She was chilled. But I was interested. But not much happened besides the odd casual meet.'

He looked to me, leaned forward and asked, 'Can I have a bite of your cake?' He continued looking at the slice of cake, giving it the importance of a panacea.

'Please do! Share in my sin', I answered.

He cut a sliver of cake on to his plate but fumbled as he ate. All the while not letting go of the coffee mug in his hands.

'Then we finished university and got jobs. In our first week at work we realised we were at the same firm.'

He smiled, almost wryly. Almost sadly.

'Weeks into work she encountered pervert behaviour. A colleague began subtly troubling her, stalking her even. She spoke to me about it. And I stood up for her. The colleague stepped back. And that changed everything between us.'

He kept glancing at my plate.

'Are you still eyeing my cake?' I asked. 'Go for it, have some more.'

'I will. I think I need a whole slice. And a smoke.'

He slouched a bit more. Then corrected his slouch and continued.

'If the way to a man's heart is through his stomach. The way to a woman's heart is through her emotions.'

'And chocolate!' I exclaimed.

'So there is truth in the stereotypes?' I asked him.

'Totally! We men look more for physical intimacy, all you women look more for an emotional anchor. Don't you?'

'I don't know about all but emotional intimacy is essential for me. Yes.' I agreed with his assessment.

'In her case, soon she started becoming all emotional about me, or so I felt. I liked her but was not looking for a commitment just then. Just some light hearted fun was what I wanted at the time. But I didn't want her to know this or I would lose her entirely I thought.' I was pleasantly astonished at his candour. 'But she, I think, started liking me and wanted more. She would send me caring messages literally every day. One day I lost it with her. I told her, it's best for her if she never messages me again.'

'She replied in one word "OK". Even though I realised her "OK" was heavy with hurt, I let it be at that too. There was more to life. And I never heard from her again.'

I was struck by the honesty. The kind of honesty that comes when we speak to ourselves, before we first hush ourselves up and then edit in relaying to others.

'Soon she left the company for another.'

'One day at a pub I learnt from common university friends that she had a tragic accident on holiday. And she died.'

'I was stunned. That day I learnt what disbelief meant.'

'Back then I wasn't sure if I wanted to be with her but I always liked her. And now, few flings later, I feel she was the best I've met – intelligent, sexy and she cared a lot for me. That much I know.'

Why do we often realise the value of what we truly treasure, in its absence? Like the value of good health, in sickness. Like the treasure of those who love us, often in their loss. I wondered.

'And I miss her. Is there any way I can tell her? That she can know?'

And the questions in my eyes met the sadness, the utter helplessness, in his.

Love Is Strength

It's New Year's Eve. I have spent my day so far at Mother Teresa's orphanage in Kolkata. I volunteered here as a schoolgirl yet today was heart wrenching. There was a room full of babies abandoned by their parents.

Why when we need a degree and a slew of interviews to get a job, do we not need any qualification – means or merit, to be a parent? Disabled children were lying in the confines of cots – no sense at all of 'the world of loved ones' leave alone of a new year coming. Some of them unable to eat or breathe normally or move or speak.

I tried something with the children – I just said, 'I love you, I love you so much,' and each one responded with a smile. EACH ONE. Some smiled in cascades, some in glimmers, some slowly, some instantly but each one's eyes smiled too.

A little boy, probably all of about three years old, with a severe injury to his head and who had his hand in bandages kept rocking in pain. But when I said smilingly, 'Do you know how handsome you are?' he erupted into a laugh. It was just magical to see his pained expression transform to laughter. Magical to see him understand and respond to love. Which means there IS clearly a language of love. Understood without boundaries. Especially by children who have yet to learn cynicism.

Today was testimony yet again, most simply yet meaningfully, to the power of love. Why then is there such a lack of love in our world? Such a scarcity? I feel privileged to have love in my life. Each of us is privileged to be love, to love, to have love. But let's remember those, especially our children who have been left out of this space of receiving love, in our prayers and in our actions of love. Love IS the greatest human strength, and the highest blessing known to human kind. Of that I'm convinced.

Someone Cares

I had returned to London after a long, 'POWerful' time in India where I was working on the children's charity Paint Our World. It was the longest I had ever been away from the U.K. since I moved there two decades ago. I had missed my friends and the joy of meeting them after a long hiatus was unmatched.

On an afternoon post my return while the sun lounged on a diaphanous bed of clouds, I met a very dear friend for lunch. It was in the midst of our working day that we took a pause, a pause for conversation. There was lots of catching up to do. Yes, there's social media and WhatsApp yet you learn that nothing compares to, or substitutes, the in–person connect.

There's no small talk. We just plunge into conversation that dances from our hearts – about all that we've been doing, why and most importantly the journey of getting to know love and ourselves better through all that we are doing and being and becoming.

The summer sun is relentless and our restaurant, typical of London, does not have air conditioning. So we decide to walk and talk post a quick lunch. Freya says she wants to tell me something but it slipped her mind.

'Don't worry, it will return to you!' I said.

As our conversation saunters along it comes back to her. And she re–members.

'It's a story, I want to tell you Priya.'

'You know that church near Borough market, I went there recently while I was in the area for some work. I was not really meant to be there but somehow was led there.'

I identify with that. London often leads me to discover spots of absolute magic and beauty when I let it lead the way. But her look was one of intense empathy that came to her all–at–once with childlike spontaneity.

'I saw a man kneeling on a pew. He seemed troubled, to be praying fervently. I have no idea who he was of course, or why he seemed so distressed. Clearly he must have been praying for things to iron out,' she told me.

My mind's eye imagined someone with a tight clasp of hands and eyes shut by the sadness life is capable of throwing at you.

'I don't know why but within minutes I found myself crying uncontrollably. As though I was fully sensing the distress of this person,' Freya continued.

Her eyes looked into mine. 'It was too much for me. I just had to leave the church.'

'You are clearly an empath. You should have sent him positive energy', I reassured her.

And she smiled, we smiled together.

'I did. I prayed fervently to God for him. I told God – I don't know what is troubling him and if his heart's desires can be fulfilled. But please show him the way to peace of mind.'

And I thought and shared with Freya, 'This is such a simple and yet simply powerful story.' For all the times we feel down and out, unloved, that no one cares, or notices or appreciates us, you never know the care, often from the most unexpected source, that lies round the bend.

Freya and I know nothing of this gentleman who was praying in distress. But we do know that a complete stranger (Freya) felt a most genuine and meaningful sense of connect with him and care for him. Whether Freya was a universe send, a God send, some serendipity or a random coincidence, it is for us to know that even in our lowest of lows when we feel life has failed us, 'reach–out' from a most unexpected source often does come our way.

The Vegetable Seller[6]

On Indian streets, colour often comes in the form of pyramids and crates of myriad fruits and vegetables. Vegetable vendors and their produce dot the roads, streets, lanes and by–lanes, in all weathers like stops on alleyways of sky. The colour also brings conversation with it as passers–by buyers haggle with the sellers who are often seen standing behind pyramids of fruits like oranges and apples or squatting on the ground with mounds of their wares of fresh vegetables before them.

This story is of one such vegetable vendor in the north Indian city of Lucknow. Lucknow is the capital of India's largest State – Uttar Pradesh. It was a salient city in Mughal India and remains, to this day, particularistic of its inheritance – a kaleidoscope of Hindu and Islamic culture, food and traditions. On a street of this bustling, fast growing syncretised city is a typical vegetable vendor. Plainly speaking, nothing of note differentiates him from his fellow vegetable sellers. He too wears the characteristic chequered lungi in banal colours of brushed white and dull blue and black. With it, a shirt in winters (unbuttoned at the top) or a vest in summers, patterned with dark patches where sweat makes its mark. A truncated pencil sits behind his ears to make note of the day's sales. Lalbhai Dev is his name.

But Lalbhai Dev is a fortunate man for, unlike other vegetable vendors, he does not have to lay his wares each day on the street, on improvised pavement level tables made of fraying tarpaulin and discarded newspapers. He has a vegetable cart. It is on wheels but he never moves it from Salaam Nawab Street where he has been from the time he was eight.

As a little boy he would help his father arrange the vegetables, dust them with an all purpose loincloth in winter and, in the summers and monsoons, he would busy himself with shooing mosquitoes and catching flies especially after the slip of crepuscular light. On some other nights he would try to snatch some street light, if the lights came on. And listen in on the English of little street boys trying to sell balloons and chewing gum to tourists who had sauntered into Salaam Nawab Street. His mother loved listening to their English, 'Mad–am, very nize balon, only tan rupees'.

During the day he would colour in big semi–used colouring books handed down to him by the lady in whose house his mother worked as a domestic help. But he would quickly get bored of colouring and join the local street boys in contiguous by–lanes in games of cricket using one of their slippers as a cricket ball. Till his father would come calling for him – sometimes with a tone of reprimand, sometimes a tone of sympathy but mostly with a tenor that belied his frustration. While he took out his frustration on his only son, the frustration he always felt was really on himself, that he was still on the vegetable cart sold to him by his uncle because he had no sons and his daughters married in villages far from Lucknow. As he grew he never dreamed of reading or writing himself, but of one day educating his children when the time would come. For this, he tried to get a spot on a better road but could not afford the monthly extortion rates demanded by the local mafia. So he stayed put on the same spot. As did the dreams for his children.

Lalbhai Dev was about fourteen years of age (he was not sure of his age or his birthday) when his father died. He had no birth certificate and just knew he was born a day before the festival of Ram Navami, that celebrates the birth of Lord Rama, the seventh reincarnation of the Hindu God Vishnu. The date is marked as per the Hindu lunar calendar so it varies each year. But Lalbhai's mother believed his birthday was the strongest omen that her son was made for great things. She believed his heart carried not just goodness, but the greatness of Lord Rama.

His father died on the floor of a government hospital in Lucknow (because beds had to be given to more urgent cases) by retching blood as he coughed. Tuberculosis killed him, the hospital said. He died of a curable disease. Only if the right drugs were administered at the right time. So he actually died of negligence. His poverty could not earn him the medical attention he needed. But his simple wife, though devastated, rattled every door to ensure her teenage son, who contracted the disease from his father, got the right medication. Lalbhai healed and returned to the vegetable cart – now in a changed role. He was the owner. No more street cricket, though he still played fly–catching to kill time when business was quiet on sullen summer afternoons. And practised his English, especially the numbers, 'Tan, ehlavan, twalve'.

He was a compliant seller often giving in to the haggling demands of his buyers. At the end of each working day he would return home and give all the money he made that day to his mother. Each day his mother waited for him to the sounds of YouTube cooking videos and with hot spiced tea and two slices of white bread. Lalbhai lived for the end of each day, to see his mother's smile, to hear her loud kiss on his forehead and her louder slurps as she drank her tea.

One day he returned home to find his mother motionless, the Samsung smartphone with a YouTube cooking channel about how to make mushroom risotto played on in Hindi as the smartphone lay in the lap of her crumpled sari. They said, it must have been a sudden heart attack.

Lalbhai was devastated. What would he go to the cart for now, who would he bring the money home to each day and who would wait for him each night? He had no bad habits, no friends and little money, so little else to do.

He grudgingly went to work each day, put on a haggling mask and now sadly and smilingly watched the flies.

One afternoon, an elderly lady stopped before his crate of bright purple brinjals. She bargained animatedly and to Lalbhai's surprise, he reciprocated animatedly. The thick waves of short hair on her head moved with her haggling–gesticulations. Her thick glasses stayed put. She wore an English dress (very unusual for Lucknow) with English sandals and spoke Hindi with a confused accent. Perhaps she spoke the English he always wanted to learn, the accented English that the foreigners spoke. Lalbhai wished to hear her accent incessantly. It carried the promise of a faraway dream.

'That's just too much for a cabbage. Forty rupees!' She said, straightening the red bow on her crisp polka dot dress.

'I'd rather buy from Royals,' she innocuously threatened.

'Madaam, these big supermarkets all carry adulterated, old vegetables. I get mine everyday. They are without chemicals.' Lalbhai was happy with himself at his response.

'Do you know what all these chemicals can do? They are too harmful to eat.'

The lady looked deliberately unconvinced but continued with both the haggling and more purchases.

Lalbhai put her shopping in a cloth bag she was carrying and volunteered to walk it to her home which was a building across the road, where she had just relocated to. When she resisted, Lalbhai insisted he help her to her building lift. There is no lift the English lady said. So leaving his wares unattended, he led her to her door carrying the vegetables she had bought, up a flight of stairs. Before he could leave she called him in, gave him some water and insisted he take a piece of cake with him and she showed him a picture of her son who lived far away – in America with his wife. As he took leave, her short white frame planted a frothy kiss on his brown petite head. And it was the first smile his heart smiled since his mother died. Across the road he returned to the same cart of vegetables, but his smile was different.

Courage Is the Answer

Indian weddings are known for their riot of colour, song, dance, fashion and food. They are not called 'big' and 'fat' for no reason! I was at one such society wedding. But to me, the greatest opulence the affluent surroundings were lit with, was the pleasant January air.

As I stood in my heavy wedding finery, plate in hand wondering which 'cuisine queue' to join, a lady I knew socially approached. She was a socialite who carried herself with swan–like elegance. While in India she has the tag of a socialite, to me she came across as quite the contrary. A no nonsense person, affirmative and warm. She may have carried the latest fashion trends but she had none of the pretentiousness associated with the socialite moniker.

We wished each other, and she asked me what I've been up to in India. The conversation inevitably turned to Paint Our World, a humanitarian project I work on. As I spoke about Paint Our World's work, about the importance of meaningful intervention and the centrality of trauma healing for children who had endured abuse, she kept looking at me with a steady gaze that harboured deep empathy. As though she knew the children or a child I was working with.

'I know what you are talking about,' she said. Her voice dipped but her tone held firm.

'I was abused as a child. Right till the time I got married.'

The lights melted away for me. I just stood stationary, plainly looking at this gorgeous lady before me, in all her splendour and elegance, in disbelief.

'What did you do about it?' I asked as the sounds of the fanfare around us dimmed in my head. I was trying to keep my voice from sounding perturbed.

'What can *you* do about it? Nothing. Even my husband I never told. Now he has a vague hint. You are the first person I'm *actually* telling.'

I stood in complete stillness. My mind – aghast. Shaking.

When I found my voice I quizzed her. 'Why didn't you out him? The abuse could have stopped.' My voice betrayed my anger at the social system that keeps a child suppressed.

'Have you lived in a joint family?'

'No'. I replied, matter–of–factly.

'Then you won't know', she said with an air of inevitable acceptance and absolute conditioning.

'He was a very respected member of the family. He was helping my parents and other family members financially too. I still meet him at family functions and have to touch his feet'.

I felt the churn of disgust in the pit of my stomach.

I quietly thought to myself, if a privileged, confident, educated woman like her has felt the institutions of the Indian family and society have accorded her no space to give voice to her abuse, without the fear of retribution, what about the average Indian woman who is often dependent on the men in her life (often she is made to be dependent socially and financially).

'But what I have done is protect my two daughters from him. I ensure they are never alone with him.' She spoke with unshakable resolve.

'These people normally have a pattern. And they will keep perpetuating the pattern if they feel there are no consequences for this', I tried to reason with her.

But she took solace that her abuse period was over and her daughters were safe.

A couple of years down the line Harvey Weinstein happened and the #MeToo campaign on social media erupted.

And it reached India. And this lady's elder daughter explicated her abuse on Facebook. And her abuser, as her mother then came to learn, was the very same 'respected, family man' who had abused her for years together all those years ago.

But it was a little too late. The man had recently died leaving the lady with devastating guilt and regret. Not so much that she had failed herself. But that she has also failed her daughter.

Courage is the only way. But the answer is courage 'now', not courage 'later'. We need to shrink the hiding places of all such perpetrators. The time is now. And the force – each one of us.

Focus

Recently a general chat with a friend who is an entrepreneur led to him sharing that his life is now all about leading his business, with a laser like focus. The Arjuna focus – where all he can see are his goals, one at a time.

This got me thinking.

Arjuna, the great hero of the Indian epic, the Mahabharata, is still revered for his unshakable, goal oriented focus. The epic is approximately five thousand years old but even today boys in India are often named after Arjuna, in the hope and belief that the child will imbibe the glorified qualities of this war hero – his valor, his skill, his focus, his handsomeness. All these qualities put together are perceived to be embodied by this one hero – the third son of King Pandu.

One of the most famous stories from the Mahabharata that elucidates Arjuna's goal oriented focus best is from his childhood. Arjuna was a prince and together with his four other brothers and hundred cousin brothers was schooled and trained in archery by a formidable teacher of that time, namely Guru Dronacharya. Those days schooling and training, especially for princes who belonged to the Kshatriya (warrior) class, was done in gurukuls. Gurukuls were spartan and rigorous residential schools where the children would be under the sole guidance and tutelage of an assigned teacher or guru.

One sunny day in the gurukul, Guru Dronacharya gave all the princes a test in archery. He asked them to shoot a bird sitting on a tree branch. Before the shooting could begin, in turn, he asked each prince what he could see. Their answers were various and included – the sky, the sun, the leaves, the branch, the tree, the bird – its feathers, its beak.

When Arjuna's turn came his answer was a mere three words: 'The bird's eye'. He said that was all that was visible to him; that is, his finite goal in its most absolute sense to the exclusion of everything else. Guru Dronacharya was most impressed. In India this story is repeatedly narrated to children to teach them what being goal oriented really means.

There is another story, this time from Arjuna's adulthood that made him the unquestionable apotheosis of what it means to owe relentless allegiance to focus. The story of how this prince won Princess Draupadi in a swayamwara. Swayamwaras were tests of skill orchestrated for eligible bachelors to contest and thereby win a princess' hand in marriage. Draupadi was known to be the most beautiful woman and princess of her time. Accordingly her swayamwara was a seemingly impossible feat for even the best of the best. A rotating fish was placed on the ceiling. The winning suitor had to pierce the fish's eye making his aim while looking into the rotating fish's reflection in a pool of water. Arjuna again, with his unparalleled focus, not only was victorious but also made it seem like a mundane task!

Yet, this valorous Arjuna, the lodestar of focus, in the battlefield of Kurukshetra, when he had to fight his cousins – the Kauravas, and other senior members of his family, loses all focus. He shudders and is unable to even pick up his bow and arrow. Leave alone fight. He is unable to fathom how to fight an army that includes those he most reveres including his teacher Guru Dronacharya and his grand–uncle Bhishma. Not only is Arjuna's focus pulverized but he loses all sense of identity and faces a crisis of meaning in life. And thereby, the holy book of the Hindus, the Holy Gita is born. The sacred Gita is a sermon by Lord Krishna to this baffled and torn Arjuna, on the battlefield of Kurukshetra.

Arjuna's earlier tests were about skill alone, where focus in itself was a complete asset. But when he was faced with a situation that called on so much more than just his skill, that called on his emotions and his ability to exercise wisdom and emotional intelligence more than his skill, he was tormented. Here, his turning to God (Lord Krishna) is what empowered him. Even in our lives, we can't reduce exercising focus to doing just that and act on it and with it singularly, to achieve results. Life asks much more of us than that. In the vicissitudes of life, our real test often lies in how best we can emotionally manage ourselves and others and then to put our skills to that management. Therein, lies the value of emotional intelligence in leading a happier, more fulfilling life.

In schools, in our educational system too, the learning of skills is privileged over understanding how best to manage the self and others especially in adverse circumstances. Then when success comes at the cost of personal happiness and health we often have Arjuna's Kurukshetra moments.

And with Arjuna, there is another learning. Even with our greatest 'heros', just as Lord Krishna reminds Arjuna in the Mahabharata, there is no all white. Or all black. They and we, are all shades of grey, in varying proportions. Arjuna even.

A Rainbow Faced Morning

It was a rainbow–faced morning in Kolkata. Or that's what the children said. Their laughter mitigated the third day of uncharacteristically incessant, December rain. When I asked them what smiles on a rainy day amounted to, the littlest girl in the front, dressed with a wide smile in her eyes said, 'Rainbow!' The other children then followed suit in a chorus after me, 'Rainbow faces', they said with magic in their little voices.

They were children from local children's charities brought together by an effervescent do–gooder. On a rainy Sunday morning, they sat huddled in smiles and happy, expectant expressions. We had all assembled for a cause. To auction their paintings created under the able stewardship of a Kolkata artist. All proceeds were to go to selected charities.

I chatted with the children before the event began. On the joy of simple things. On the wings of a butterfly one had drawn. And what a horse's eyes once said to another. And the care of dolphins. The story of how dolphins saved a swimmer from the threat of a shark by encircling him in a circle of love and protection. The kind of conversations that life ought to be about. The conversations we lose on the way to adulthood. The ones we sacrifice for the maze of bigger dreams. The joy of simple things and simple smiles, standing forgotten. Often to our detriment.

I was there that morning on the organiser's behest to auction the paintings. A singer brought everyone together in a festive rendition of Christmas Carols. It was all about the togetherness of Christmas, the love of giving, the joy of adults learning from children.

The auction was the centre stage of the event. It unfolded with tremendous energy. Little Kadinskys, Matisses, Monets and Turners were picked up by Calcuttans for charity. The auction was set in three phases. The first two phases were the auction of paintings made by the children of two charities. The third set of artworks were of children from privileged backgrounds who donated the money their paintings fetched at the auction, to charity.

Being the auctioneer, with every artwork, my eyes travelled through the gallery to encourage bids. But a particular person, commanded my attention in my role as the auctioneer. She bid for, and won the bid for, a majority of the children's paintings.

She wore her sharply cut salt and pepper tresses with elegance. And a starkly simple *salwaar kameez* to go with it. She wore no make-up and her glasses did not belie the thoughts behind her constant expression. In other words, she wore simplicity and a simple confidence. She was a serious bidder. If a painting was slow to pick up, her bid would step in and be the 'pick me up'. With other paintings, when the price seemed set at 'sold' her bidding banner would make a quiet, assertive presence and initiate a new bidding dynamic. I was the auctioneer, but her bids were the steer. People seemed intrigued by this inscrutable bidder.

Post the auction I was speaking to a friend. Just then I noticed the 'serious bidder', now the owner of many of the children's artworks, at the far corner of the room. I asked my friend if she knew who she was. She did not. So I went up to the lady and before I could introduce myself, she graciously complimented my role as the auctioneer effusively. 'You were very good,' she said. 'You engaged people in the process very well'.

'Thank you, I'm humbled', I answered as I introduced myself and congratulated her on her 'meaningful art haul', still wondering who she was.

She reciprocated by introducing herself as Roma, a Kiwi visiting family in Kolkata. She had worked in India in her youth but had since retreated to a beautiful spot in New Zealand (a place her heart always wanted to be in) where she was dabbling in projects that held meaning for her. Offbeat things. Experiences that the tapestry of meaning are made of. Meaning that we often elide in our everyday lives because we are conditioned to run from meaningful experiences towards shinier things.

One of her sentences struck me most, 'I own four outfits. I feel that's more than enough.' But yet when it came to buying children's artwork for a beautiful cause, she delved most deeply into her pocket and spent most magnanimously.

Now that's what I call an 'on–beat' life. And here was a lady, living it!

Here's to the people we meet who show us that not only is it ok to be off (or rather on) beat, but it's actually quite magical to do your own thing and to be your own self. And here's to each of us being just that.

There Is Someone
for Each of Us

I would always greet Sara with smiling eyes. And she would return my smile each time with a lift of wing.

I loved the attention to detail that she extended to ensure the well-being of everyone who came to the fitness centre. She was in-charge of the ladies' changing area. From ensuring lockers were properly locked and members remembered to take their keys as they sprinted off to gym; to handing them a bottle of mineral water and ensuring clean towels and shower caps were ready as they returned post their workout.

Sara's sense of nurture pervaded in even the most mundane tasks she had to do. Sometimes it is the smallest acts of nurture that really matter the most in our daily lives. And when they go missing or we forget to do it for ourselves, their absence becomes the 'big things'. The absence pervades our life, like another person – a faraway person, whom we miss but can't see. It colours our mood and our interactions with ourselves and with others, and we shift our focus to hankering after the big things, missing the point – that actually it is the small things that we need, that we are missing.

One morning when the skies outside did not know whether to smile or to cry and the changing area was quiet, Sara came up to me smiling and said, 'Ma'am, you know so many members are here everyday. But I look forward to your coming here the most. Tell me why?' She asked curiously, like a child from the eighties ready to delve into a Tell Me Why encyclopaedia.

'I'm always happy to see you too Sara,' I responded.

'It's your energy I think Ma'am. Everyone comes in a hurry but you also stop and smile.'

It was a life affirming feeling for me to know that my little gestures were noticed in a way that made a positive difference. My smiles were a response to a smile that smiled at all but rarely got a smile back.

'You look after us all so well Sara. I really hope you enjoy being here.'

'It's okay now but I was not meant to be here.'

My expression asked a question. She 'heard' it and answered.

'Women in my home don't work. We are poor people from outside the city no Ma'am. I take a bus, three autos and then walk to get here.'

'How long does that take?' I asked with admiration.

'If I'm lucky I'm here in two hours,' she said while folding and separating the laundered towels.

'I'm the youngest. All my siblings are elder, married and in their own homes. When my father died there was so much problem on my mum. So without asking anyone, I told two friends who had left for the city to find me a job. With their help only I got this.' She looked relived and sad at the same time.

'But now people in my locality say no nice boy will marry me. Because I left home on my own to work. Because I leave home everyday and return at night.'

Her petite frame stood still. Before I could respond to refute these 'people' who come of no good to help meaningfully but are prompt with their regressive judgements, the chuckle returned in Sara's eyes and she said, 'But you know what my mum says?'

'Tell me.' I smiled.

'She says God has made a partner for everyone. So in life, I can go out and work and do what I believe in and yet there will be a man for me. The right man for me.'

We smiled together. Of a story we shared. Our different lives met wonderfully at this story.

And she asked, 'Ma'am, are you married?'

'I'm not.'

'You don't want to get married? I hear a lot of women nowadays don't want to.'

'I've just not found a guy I connect with yet, to share my life with.' I replied, matter–of–factly.

She looked bemused. Then she said with parental assurance and sweetness, 'I believe my mum. There is someone for each one – who will respect you for who you are, and support you to be who you want to become.'

And our eyes met in knowing smiles.

Birthday Lessons

It's just over a week past my Birthday. This year especially, my Birthday became an excuse for a thread of experiences, the kind that catch your heart and make a space in it. My heart is awash with gratitude yet it's a somewhat mixed bag. A mixed bag of feelings.

There's the joyful reminiscence of a Birthday surprise, indelibly put together with love.

A friend as dear to me as melody is to song, led me with the mastery of her love, to a gathering of our closest friends. I'm in a puddle of smiles as I recall her sway of tactful starlight, how she got me to change my outfit into something nicer and got me to rearrange my day without any clue whatsoever that there was a surprise waiting in the wings. The sight of a group of my dearest friends, as I walked in to one of my favourite restaurants in Delhi most unsuspectingly, was a feeling that no amount of money can ever buy. It was a feeling that only lots of love enables. The balloons, the specially crafted ten layer Birthday cake, the laughter, were all memory deposits that shape a heart. Then my Birthday celebrations in Kolkata were unforgettable too – the most treasured souls I know in the City of Joy came together in celebration in advance of my Birthday as I would be away on the day. And my neighbours with their surprise Birthday cake and song for me. And fun filled celebrations with the beautiful Paint Our World children. Yet amidst all this merry making and love is also the story of a friendship going amiss.

An old friend chose the time of my Birthday, without the whiff of even a misunderstanding, to remind me that bonds in India are forged only by family ties. Friendships that lie outside the blood–scape of family are essentially just name–sakes, her words and behaviour made unequivocal. While I was determined to not let one sad experience mar all the Birthday joy that had come my way, I did reflect on soul connects, on my belief in their existence. Are they for real? Do they exist? Or are they myths we feed ourselves? Or coping mechanisms through an essentially uncertain and vulnerable human existence? Is blood family actually the only real thing for most people?

Just then a dear friend asked me out for coffee. And made it into yet another Birthday celebration for me replete with extremely thoughtfully and thought provokingly, chosen gifts! Over our cuppas we were chatting about how God shows up. And a little girl, probably all of three came running to our table, looking at me saying 'massii' (mother's sister). Her mother came running after her, 'I'm so sorry, she thinks you are her masi.'

'This is not masi, Navya.' Navya was emphatically told.

But little Navya chose to remain oblivious to the telling. And continued smiling her masi–smile for me. Only when her mother forcibly dragged her from my table her smile turned into a burst of tears.

If only we could extend even a small percentage of our smiles and love we reserve for blood families and, more so, for our children to others too, the tenor and colour of our world would be vastly changed. It would become more magical for each of us. Just like the effect of Navya's masi–smile for me.

The Power of Mortality

I'm at St. Mary's hospital in Paddington London. St. Mary's is part of British folklore now because it has been home to both Princesses – Diana and Kate, when they gave birth.

In popular British culture this hospital has become synonymous with the paparazzi and with the arrival of royal heirs!

But my experience here today is different. Hospitals are humbling places. They are real. Gritty–real. The mortality of life – both sides of it – birth and death – come alive here. New life and the joy and dreams, apprehension and expectation, celebration and family that come with it, are a part. But the ebb of life is as much a parcel.

As I wait for my appointment, which incidentally is just by the Lindo Wing, which welcomes new life and has welcomed the last two generations of royal heirs, I see a lady on a mobile bed. She is possibly my age. Or a little older. A live–able age. Not a die–able age. Her face is frail, rock frail. Her eyes unblinking, in a sense the unusualness of it was making it seem ominous. But somewhere also lay the serenity of cessation and the sadness that we all fight death with because life is what we are familiar with and attached to.

Her bed was wheeled away.

And then came another wheelchair with a man who had just lost his leg. The sight of blood was hard to bear. As he was wheeled in some people were casually chatting, fretting that the weather had suddenly turned gloomy. The presence of the sun had lately become such a constant that they were discussing how unprepared they were for this bout of rain and had left their umbrellas at home.

I wondered if the change in weather made any sense to a man who would re–emerge from the hospital without a limb? How relative problems are, how contextual perspective is. Was he in pain, I wondered. If so, how come his expression was so unflinching?

Before I left I thanked a member of staff and said, 'I hope that lady's okay?' I was referring to the unblinking lady on the stretcher. Hospitals in the U.K. never speak about patients, as health records are strictly confidential. So my question was more rhetorical, to placate myself really. Just then I overheard a staff member behind the desk tell another, 'She has passed away. Her family need to be informed.'

And mortality stared at me in the face. The repertoire of human excesses – that often inform all of our time on earth – the lust for fame, money and power all carry no traction, absolutely no clout in the face of nature. Yet we succumb to it all with such ease entirely forgetting the power of mortality along the way.

The power of mortality really is about living well because we are not here forever even though we live our lives as though we are. The best way to face the truth of mortality is to live full of joy and love for ourselves and others. It is in our interests that others are joyful too. If they are bitter, it is likely to spill out in their interactions with us and that will sully our experience of life.

At the hospital I reaffirmed to myself with renewed conviction what I often affirm – always glow, for the light of your soul is that of the stars. Always be humble, for your body that houses it, is shaped from dust.

Carpe Diem

A trip to India after a while in London saw me catching up with friends. One pleasant winter's evening in Kolkata I was going to meet a dear friend. I had been excited from the day before and was really looking forward to seeing her.

We were meeting at an open air, fairly new eatery. When she entered we hugged like beautiful friends do. We were both all animated to meet each other and had lots of catching up to do.

We ordered a virgin hot toddy and some kebabs. After the theatre of the toddy was over (the burning of the clove struck orange, the squeeze of the lime, the stir of the honey), we slouched back. Hot drink in hand and conversation awaiting, my friend Bridgette reached out for her phone.

Bridgette is a happening entrepreneur and a trailblazer in the beauty industry in the city of Kolkata. Following on from our appreciative exclamations of the lovely restaurant we were in, she said, 'I have to tell you all about my trips to California. Let me show you the pics.'

'I saw some pics on Facebook', I recalled, 'but I'm waiting to hear all about it from you, first–hand!'

She began scrolling through images of a working holiday that dreams are made of. Her destination was Malibu where God and man both do it best. It is where the promise of the blue oceans and even bluer skies meet the glamour of Hollywood ocean front villas.

Bridgette was in Malibu to learn the latest developments in the beauty industry.

All the images she showed me, unsurprisingly, had the shine of the sun and the whiff of Hollywood.

She led me by the hand and took me through each image telling me the story of this couple who owned this novel beauty brand and who had invited her. Through the photos, she took me through her beauty course held at this couple's luxurious home, made of opulent indoors and sun outside; and glimpses of playing dolphins and whales in the ocean waters that their magical home overlooked. Finally there was an image of this couple – kissing each other as they toasted to all those who had come from far and wide to attend the course.

'Can you believe this house?' Bridgette's beautiful hazel eyes lit up as she asked. 'It's Hollywoodesque,' I replied.

'I had such an amazing time. The house, the couple, the course, the weather, the ocean, the food, it was just a dream. Really.' She paused.

'And then, let me tell you, you won't believe what happened.'

I was waiting for another 'Hollywood–episode'. But she showed me an image of rubble to the ground. Dust. Earth. Ashes. Skeletal rubble.

'That's their house now,' she said, her face fallen. 'Just about a month after I was there. Burned by the Malibu fires.' Singed to the ground. Nothing left of it, not a trace of any memory of its erstwhile grandeur, were it not for the photographs. Just the nothingness and emptiness and noise of rubble.

The Californian fires were the worst in its history. It obscured even the sun and ate eighty–six people alive.

Then she showed me the FB post of the gentleman who had hosted them, whose home it once was. In it he wrote with courage, fortitude and grace and gave gratitude to all those who had offered support at this 'devastating time'.

We read about such tragedies in the news. But when it comes before you in someone you know, or through someone you know, the tragedy takes on a life all of its own. Way beyond news headlines.

The before and after images of this house were such stark learning. Life is a relay – we must enjoy it while it lasts. There is no guarantee of permanence. Of impermanence, there is. Let the lesson of impermanence mean we make the most of every moment, every experience. The good. And the bad. They both are teachers that come with expiry dates. Just as we do.

Love in a Practical World

The stars played in full view. Their playground was the skies of the vast grounds of the Isha Ashram. The Isha Ashram in Coimbatore, South India, has been conceptualised by Sadhguru – a visionary of immeasurable clarity who refers to himself as a mystic.

Just beyond the ashram gates, a slate grey sculpture of Lord Shiva, absolute and majestic, presides over vast fields of green. Beyond the flat fields lies the verdant green of the undulating Velliangiri Hills. Surveying it all is the Lord Shiva statue. Shiva, the Hindu God who symbolises the destruction of excess is also referred to as Adiyogi or the ultimate *yogi* (ascetic). Serenading the Adiyogi, chants of the Saptarishi Aarti[7] reverberated in the air. The Saptarishis were seven sages in ancient times and this aarti is believed to have been handed down from them, through millennia. I was told, I was privileged to be at the ashram at the time of this aarti. But my real learnings lay elsewhere, in simple conversations.

Aarti and prasad over, I began walking towards the ashram with a friend I had made there. We chatted about every day–

ness; about applying our learnings to life; about making the abstract, practical. Just then we bumped into a couple I had befriended a day before. And with them a German monk.

We stood at the bend of the gently winding road that finds its way into the inner sanctum of the ashram that houses the meditation centre (the Dhayana Linga). A diaphanous layer of cloud sat high. The moon sat above it. Each time the clouds moved, the moon yawned. The palm combs shimmered with each moon–yawn. Below the tall betel palms, in our significant insignificance, we exchanged pleasantries that slowly, with ease, led to a more meaningful conversation.

This couple were fairly young and had chosen to give up their 'glittering' careers in London to relocate to the ashram as full time volunteers. One thing that struck me about my time at the ashram was that each individual seemed to be on their own journey wherein the relationship centric insecurities, that we normally see playing out in society and which are, more so, strikingly pronounced in Indian society – of 'my' husband, 'my' wife, 'my' child, 'my' parent, 'my' sibling, were less palpable there.

I asked them how they both seemed in such incredible sync, that as a young couple they both made this 'life changing decision' together to surrender to spiritual life over worldly life.

Then the lady, Leela began telling me her story. A most life affirming, relationship affirming one, especially in an era when Apples and Oranges have turned into electronic devices that I see some of my friends use to keep tabs on their partners.

Leela sauntered into easy conversation about her bond with the ashram; of how when she enrolled on the three month Hatha Yoga course at the ashram, she made a conscious decision to disconnect from the wider world. This included suspending all communication with her loved ones, including her family and her husband for the entire three months. They had the ashram's number in case of an emergency. She chose to do this not because she didn't love them. Much to the contrary, she loved them enough to want to work on herself; to focus on her inner work such that when she emerged from it she would hopefully be more joyful and mindful about the gift of life, of herself and of each role she played.

This is clearly easier said than done, I thought. Three months of NO contact!

I asked, 'How did your parents and husband react?'

Leela smiled, the smile that a day before led me to pay her a compliment from which our friendship began its blossom. A smile that said, 'I love life'. The best make up one could have.

'He understood', she replied, her petite frame briefly looking up at her husband.

'It was what she wanted to do', he said in his gentle voice and soft British accent.

'You know what it was Priya', Leela's tenor carried intrigue, 'It was everyone else who was aghast. 'My friends and everyone said, what are you doing? You might emerge from the three months and find Sachin's gone. He has left you for another.'

'I can imagine everyone telling you that. Or that you are shirking your responsibilities of being a wife by going so far away to do your own thing and in your own way,' I said.

And then what happened post the three months? Did their marriage survive? Was their love imperilled in any way? Most relationships that I'm aware of might falter with a high probability that a new love interest might emerge in such an absence.

This story, however, has a learning that challenges all conventional wisdom that often leads to relationships becoming about clipping wings rather than about giving oneself and one's partner the space to span your wings. It has a beautiful learning, that I take heart, and a love lesson, from. Leela returned so positively transformed to a partner who loved and respected her as much now as he did three months before. Their love thrives and today they stood before me radiating their love to so many more, including me. With moon yawns and the Ashram Air bearing witness.

Whose Checklist Are You Living By?

It's Valentine's Day but that's not the reason why the day will become memorable for me.

The lead up to V Day was especially powerful this year. I had organised a cruise party on the River Hooghly in Kolkata for the Paint Our World children and seeing their joy was infectious and life affirming. And then on the Day itself the children got sports shoes as part of a sneakers drive made possible by people loving–heartedly coming forward to make this happen. Later in the day, a friend suggested we meet for dinner at a city club. I was leaving the city soon and seeing her would be the icing to my day. From being with the children, I made my way to the club looking forward to unwinding by sharing with Diya.

The evening had a song in its air. That time of year when the Kolkata weather Gods get it just right. When the air is the blink of a gentle breeze become still.

Meeting Diya is always a joy. Nimble, unpretentious, and as clear hearted as water, is how she is.

We decided to sit outdoors – in the blink of the still breeze. And we began chatting as connected friends do. We spoke about myriad things – and a lot about learning, and self–growth.

And then, Diya shared a powerful story with me.

Like for every parent, when her teenage son was applying to go to university in the U.S.A it came with its own share of apprehension for her. Yet how this story unfolded, on one hand, it would make you think it is the stuff that Bollywood films are made of. On the other hand, it is made of the soul song that each of our lives really ought to comprise of.

Her son Armaan is a phenomenal squash player. He also has a glowing academic track record. As a result of both he got an ED (early decision) place (scholarship included) at a prestigious U.S. university. But Armaan's dream was an Ivy League university. With ED if you reject your place, it will give you learning but not a second chance, often like life itself.

Yet, this teenager, with clear soul–ed clarity chose to take the risk. The risk that he may not get a place in the coveted Ivy League institutions and be without the option of reverting to the envious ED place he has been offered earlier. His family was anxious. They all, in their own ways, attempted reasoning with him that it's best he does not take the risk. It's best he settles for this ED offer.

Then one evening Armaan went to his mum. He sat her down, took her hand lovingly in his and looking into her eyes he said, 'Mum if you put pressure on me, you know I might give in. But I don't want to take up this ED place. My dream is the Ivy League and I'm willing to take the risk and will even settle for a city college in India if I have to as a result.' This seventeen year old understood the risk he was taking to realize his dream might lead him to a reverse reality. He well understood the checklist his friends and concerned family were putting to him. But he chose his own 'inner check list' at a time when the outcome was unknown to him. These are the times when self belief *really* comes into play – not in the supreme confidence that you will get what you want but in the quiet confidence that, in the process of realizing your dreams, you will tackle whatever challenges come your way, with inner conviction.

The outcome – he is today at the Ivy League university he dreamed about. This would have never happened had he 'settled' for his EC College place; if he had not stood his ground in the face of pressure. Yes, it's a Bollywood ending. But it could have gone the other way. Had the Ivy League place not come through his options would have been between a tier 3 American college or a university back home in India. Yet, even if plan C would have been his only remaining choice, he would have been an all–out winner. A winner, because even at the impressionable age of seventeen, he listened to, and understood, his inner voice over that of everyone else's counsel and conditioning. Whatever the outcome would have been, his victory lay in his choosing to live life on his own terms. What's more meaningful in life, but to live this journey authentically, determined by our own script?

Each of our lives is about stories, about our stories. But how many of these stories do we consciously, with full awareness, of our 'inner voice' choose for ourselves? And how many of these stories or their trajectories are determined by our conditioning; of our concerns of what others will say or how we will be judged at large? Our story, each day, has to be reclaimed. Each of us owes this much to ourselves to reclaim our story for ourselves. But why is 'this reclaiming' or, in other words, living our authentic life so vital? It is fundamentally important because it helps you get more of what you want in life. Being less authentic helps you get what others want of you in life.

Yet we often relegate being authentic to the back because the process of being authentic might mean that at times or at many a time you won't be conforming to the status quo. Conforming is not just about the pressure to fit in on the outside – how you dress, walk, talk, eat, socialize but the most crushing pressure is felt when there is a need to conform from within; when you are not entirely in agreement with, convinced by, or believe in, what you are conforming to. This creates stress and inhibitions. It lowers self–esteem. It takes away from self–confidence. It clouds your clarity; your sense of direction and purpose in life. When we try and identify with what we are not we create a fictional self. This causes stress because there is a constant tension between who we are and who we are portraying ourselves to be. Whereas with being authentic, though you might challenge people around you, your life path becomes clearer. The process will bring up challenges. But life is a bag of challenges anyways so why not make a conscious decision to take on those challenges that are truest to yourself because in taking on these challenges you gift yourself the greatest opportunities for self growth; for you to author your life instead of living a life that succumbs to the dictates of society – that though is meant to enable us often ends up having a 'disabling' affect on us.

The journey is yours, not of others to live through you. So reclaim it to make it your fulfilling journey. And as Nietzsche said, if when you dance people think you are mad, it's just that they can't hear the music.

The Backstory to Success

It was a crisp spring afternoon in London. Halfway in bloom cherry blossoms kept watch on me, on a tree lined high street. A chauffeur driven car soon arrived to pick me from the tube station. The drive was short. We passed by unassuming little shops and corner shops. Then vastness that was met with a huge construction. Though Goliathan in structure, the entrance to it was small and modest.

I was warmly welcomed and led through a short labyrinth of stairs and corridors till we came to a long corridor at the end of which was the office of the gentleman I was here to meet. The gentleman was on the phone. Seeing me outside his office door he smiled and warmly gesticulated for me to come in.

It was a plush office – beautiful leather crafted sofas complemented the stature of the office desk and chairs. It was already a big office and the surround glass windows gave it a sense of being even bigger. I was here to meet Rami Ranger CBE, the Founder of Sun Mark, an international marketing and distributing company which has the marketing of several household brands across the globe, under its belt. I've been fortunate to have Rami Uncle as my mentor.

One of the stalwarts of the British Indian community, his innate humility belies his accomplishments. Each time we meet, I'm struck by his imperturbable humility – I've realised humility comes to him as naturally as a sunflower's turn to the sun.

He gives me a book and we get drawn into conversation. Then he remembers ours is a lunch meet and in his characteristically warm, avuncular manner he interrupts.

'First you tell me what will you eat? There is nothing around here', he says, 'Except for a Subway and an MnS food.'

'What would you like to have Uncle?' I ask.

'I will have my usual, a sandwich from MnS,' he smiles, adjusting his blazer.

'Then may I request for an MnS vegetarian sushi platter? We can share?' I replied.

He tells his staff ordering the lunch, 'Please, ask everyone else (the staff in the open plan area his office overlooks) what they would like.' And we lapse back into conversation.

It is my first time in Rami Uncle's office. Framed certificates of his myriad achievements as a leading entrepreneur in Britain, a philanthropist and as a stalwart of the British Indian community, bedecked the walls around us.

Yet the conversation this time, is not about him per say. Rather it's about him by circumlocution. It's about his sojourn not as a business tycoon or a lodestar of his community. It's about his journey as a child born to a self–empowered mother way back in 1947.

The story of his mother inspires such that it gives an incredible insight into his tenor of tenacity, humility and success.

Rami Ranger was one of midnight's children. He was born in 1947, the year India achieved Independence from the British. It was also the year India was bloodily partitioned into India and Pakistan. The unprecedented, acrimonious mass migration of people that followed, saw a blood bath that led to a million deaths.

Born in July 1947, Rami Ranger arrived on the eve of India's independence on 15 August that year and also on the eve of the gruesome partition. He was the posthumous child of his father who was martyred in India's freedom struggle. He had seven brothers and sisters before him. He was born in what is present day Pakistan. His beautiful young mother was widowed with seven children and while carrying the eighth one. Post her husband's untimely demise she was relentlessly cajoled to give her children up for adoption. Family and friends perpetually discouraged her to even attempt raising her children as they believed it was unequivocal that she would not possibly be able to bring eight children up single–handedly.

Yet, his mother not only moved with her seven young children and an infant across the border to India during one of the most frightening times recorded in human history but also battled the stigma of widowhood at a tender age and made a most courageous decision to raise her children by herself. Despite the 'thought and speak at large' she remained adamant and heroically vehement at being the mother to her children no matter what.

Rami Uncle paused as we reminisced about her. He smiled quietly at me and asked, 'If my mother had put me into an orphanage, do you think I would be here today?' And I looked down at the book and then up at him, 'Uncle, your story of success is a testimony to the stubbornness of your mum's love for all of you.'

'And each of my brothers and sisters is a success story. Each one has done well for himself and herself,' he continued.

'I'm glad to know your mum through you.' I felt blessed to be hearing her story first hand from Uncle.

The certificates on the walls around me now carried added significance. I saw a mother's indomitable spirit, despite extreme hardship, pieced together in them. On my right hand side, right beside the sofa was a glass showcase. Within it was a cake that had been mummified. It was Mrs. Ranger's birthday gift to her husband on his seventieth Birthday. It carried the swagger and success of his story – a Bentley (of which Rami Uncle is a proud owner); a book (one that he has authored about his life); a globe (signifying the global reach of his company Sun Mark) and astride it all a trophy (connoting the many awards he has received from Her Majesty, The Queen). This is the front story of success, of his success. As with all success stories, we are often taken in by the glamour; by the sheen achieved; in the process often forgetting every story has a backstory – and that is where the real learning lies. In fact, every single story, whether one of overarching success or failure, carries a backstory where the conditioning happens and the outcome takes shape. For is even villainy not often a successor to the backstory of victimhood? And it is in these backstories that invaluable learning resides and in how we deal with them, life is determined.

Here's a heartfelt salute to Rami Uncle's mother – may her example live on to inspire many, many more.

And before I left, Uncle made me privy to a file that lay in a cupboard behind his office chair. That's where the real treasures lay – his letters of appreciation from his first employers in the U.K. Like a letter from Curry's commending him for achieving above target sales. The file contained a queue of such letters with Uncle giving me honoured access to read through each of them.

'I started my business with two pounds', he said, watching me engrossed in the letters. 'Now I have a Bentley. Then I could not even afford a cycle. I've worked very hard Priya.'

And I saw the smile that comes from a life of hard work shift to his eyes.

Where Does God *Really* Live?

I had arrived into Kolkata at the tail end of spring. Before the heart of summer hits, the city is lashed by intense spells of wind, rain, thunder and lightning – called the nor'westers. At this time of year the sun quickly climbs up to its peak and then it descends on a stairway of clouds. And this stairway dissipates into torrential downpours. At one such time, amidst this scene, some little souls wondered where God *really* lives.

I reached the premises of Paint Our World shortly after a nor'wester spell. The air smelt of moist, rain–drenched earth. Nature carried this fragrance of nostalgia into a spot of soul. This post rain Kolkata air is one of the things I miss in London. Kolkata does not have the sea or the mountains and in the midst of queues of buildings greenery jostles for space. Nature is at a premium. But at these times, despite the pollution, the air carries the ineluctable speak of nature.

It was early evening and time for the younger children to begin their Paint Our World art workshop. They had no idea I was in town. I wished to surprise them. So I decided to go into the classroom and meet them before their class began. My plan was to sit through the class with them and then spend some quality time creating memories with song and dance, as they love both. And we have our favourites that we sing to, and dance on, together.

When they saw me they came running. Soon I had little souls clinging to my waist. Two of the little ones managed, from the balcony just outside the classroom, to spread the word that I was in house! And within a minute the elder children thronged the classroom door.

As I was chatting with the older children, the little ones adorably instructed me, 'Priya Didi don't look towards the classroom or the blackboard'.

'You have a workshop in a few minutes', I reminded them. 'Sir (the workshop teacher) is here.'

'We will finish in two minutes', they implored in angelic voices.

And literally in the space of two minutes I was asked to bend down, two little palms were placed on my eyes, and then removed for the 'reveal'. Two drawings that tugged at my heart were on the blackboard. An ice cream and a book. What was written within the drawings tugged at my heart strings even more.

Little Aasha said, 'Didi, you are not the only one who can surprise us. We also want to surprise you.' Another little

Angel holding my little finger, looked up at me saying, 'because you will feel happy, just like we are feeling happy.'

The ice cream said, 'We miss you very much Priya Didi and we love you Priya Didi'.

The book read, 'Water is water, water is blue O my Priya di we love you very much.'

And then the book was signed 'from your lovely children.' While each word was invaluable to me, their signature spoke with the most life–affirming tenor. For over five years I have been working with this group of children, some of whom were around two years old when I began working with them. I work with the hope that they are imbibing each day that they are loved very much. But this signature was most revelatory to me; telling me that they know how special and prized they are in general and know how much their smiles and well being matters to me such that they have come to *feel* that they are 'my children'. And not just 'my children' but 'my lovely children', that is, they are growing with a happy self–esteem and a meaningful confidence about their loveliness.

This experience adds to our bouquet of most meaningful times together. But little did I realise the resonance for us all and life learning, especially for me, that was to come via our post art class conversation.

Class over, the children decided they first wanted to have a family chat, that is, speak to me. The song and dance they said would happen after that. They had just gone to new classes and were full of stories that their little minds were brimming with and that they wanted to share – of their new classroom; teachers; books; friends. Most of all, my focus was on how they were feeling about these new things.

As we were sharing, they wanted to know about me too. In particular four year old Joy asked, 'Can't you get here by train? Would that cost less money? Then you can be with us more.'

I explained to Joy because of the oceans that lie between India and the U.K. one has to take a plane, to fly over the waters.

Veena animatedly shared her wisdom with us all, 'You know Didi I've seen a plane so many times in the sky. It was so small.' She showed its smallness in a centimetre her forefingers and thumb made. 'Then before I came here one day I was taken to a road near the airport. And then I saw a plane that came over me. And it looked soooooo big.' Both her hands opened to where a hug begins to show the bigness this time.

'And what did you learn from this Veena?' She looked at the other littler children and then at me, 'What we see from far is not the same as what we see from near.'

An older girl added to her wisdom, 'Never judge from afar. Things are not always what they seem to be. We must remember that always'.

Just then Sana wished to know, 'Priya Didi, have you ever seen clouds from the plane?'

'Yes, almost every time I'm on a plane I see clouds. First the clouds are above. Then as the plane climbs higher they become at eye level. Finally, when the aircraft completes its ascend, many times I feel I am flying on a carpet of clouds.'

'Did you see God's house among the clouds?' Joy asked wonderingly.

'You know where I see God's house?' I asked her.

All the children suddenly went quiet for a few seconds with a look that said little thinking caps were put on.

Seven year old Devika then spryly stood up and her excitement ended the 'thinking silence', 'Here, with us all. With big, happy family!'

'How did you know?' I asked.

'Didi you say no, I see God's smile when you smile. And I see God cry when you cry. So I knew from that.' She said with a matter of fact smile that was happy at her deduction.

And my eyes smiled a smile. And Devika smiled and each of the other children too. And together we smiled the truest God shaped smile.

And that smile lives in my heart.

So where does God *really* live?

The Ice Cream Van

The Bernese Swiss Alps are distinctively magical. When I checked into my room at the Alpina Gstaad, from my balcony, they peered at me like the tops of melting vanilla ice cream cones. That was when the sun yawned at them. The following morning, rain clouds swirled around their stillness like planets orbiting a pyramid sun. And between torrential downpours when the sun chose to shine in short, sharp, intense spells, it lit the mountain tops with diamond tiaras. This Alpine magic not only pervades but seeps into the very fabric of the Alpina – not in the unsurprising ways of a swish ski resort but in strikingly surprising ways.

In the surprising ways of an Ice Cream Van.

The Ice Cream Van sits adroitly in the hotel's front yard. It's cheerful and happy and vibrant on the outside. As ice cream vans typically are. Yet it's anything but a stereotypical ice cream van. It belies what lies on the inside. A powerhouse of connectivity with work at the grassroots' level on empowering causes in hotspots around the world making it quite a curiously unprecedented inhabitant of an uber luxurious ski resort.

It is the 'heart–child' of my friend Nachsom Mimran – who lives life heart shaped. A half way between Johnny Depp and Russell Brand in looks, his charisma is all his own. His acute awareness and insane honesty about his vulnerabilities, which the best of us work to mask about ourselves, is disarming. And his spirit of nurture makes one feel like one is home.

One late afternoon, as the most extravagant cars made a beeline for the Alpina's front porch, Nach, as he is fondly called, ushered me into the van with the childlike zeal of Alice taking me by the hand into 'Wonderland'.

Nach's eyes begin pointing to the van much before we reach it. They light up with stories of what the van is all about – connecting do–gooders to each other (whom Nach has ascribed the moniker of 'creative activists') working courageously, creatively and assiduously in different parts of the world to create meaningful change in areas such as sustainability; house building; education; health care etc.

Switzerland is a safe, chic country and Gstaad a lodestar for the best of Swiss chic and ease. Such is the aura of its wealth and serenity – in its natural beauty and in the predisposition of its people, that when the landscape sinks in, the brittleness of the world just evaporates. Nach, though in this ensconce, chooses to immerse himself in finding creative ways to connect the brittleness of the world with the calm opulence inscribed in Switzerland.

Inside the van Nach shows me how the connectivity happens. A laptop sits astride the table and takes center stage together with images of the 'creative activists' pasted above the van's windows. Reference is made to which of the United Nation's seventeen Global Goals, for our world to achieve by 2030, the images relate to. A bench encircles the laptop and a Skype connection takes us to creative activists working in different countries. We connect with a creative activist who is a taxi driver in Uganda. While driving his taxi he is so engrossed in updating us about his 'work on the ground' that, at first, he misses noticing Nach. When he does notice him, he is simply delighted.

I sense a child like excitement brewing in me alongside deep respect for Nach and the creative activist we are speaking to.

The Ice Cream Van understands that the skies do not divide up to the borders of nation states. It profoundly knows how the very sensibility of our planet does not recognize this divvying up we humans have engineered. It knows that it is our very own indiscretions, that the planet is now revolting, as a whole to. Challenges we face need compassion, imagination and courage. Courage where vulnerability is strength. I want to understand where Nach's deep knowing of this comes from. In other words, the roots and route of the love he so consciously knows and spreads. And I learn, it seeds from a story, a simple story from his childhood.

We speak about his mother. Her loss. Tragically in a riding accident in South America. She was gone too soon. And from the womb of this conversation the story of love emerges.

He was all of six when he was walking on a street in Dakar, the capital of Senegal, with his mother. He was struck by a sight he saw and vividly recalls to this day. Poor people sitting on the side of a street playing board games, chatting and having a whale of a time. He wondered how come, despite such penury, they were happy? They seemed to have no cares in the world. And he quizzed his mother about this.

His mother replied, 'Why don't you spend some time with them?' She wanted her son to find out for himself.

Nach looked at the bunch of *Together Bands* on his wrist and then back at me, 'So I did just that. I spent time with them. And I realized you really don't need to be rich in the sense of money to be happy. And this realization changed everything for me.'

I sensed his mother's love pervade the ice cream van. His Dakar experience with his mother and the street side people was a seed. Its blossom – The Ice Cream Van. And how can there not be truth to the statement – love never dies.

The Nose Stone[8]

Her nose stone had a beauty all of its own. The thin gold like plate it sat on was all jagged but each time Bubna wore the stone it shone on her like a teardrop on a lip.

It was her good luck charm. She began wearing it suddenly one day and her husband asked where she got it from, was she having an affair on the pretext of going out to work? She replied, 'It's the diamond my parents gave me when I got married. That I safely kept away.'

'Diamond? Your parents gave yooouu? That you kept away?'

Her husband, emaciated and inebriated, was satiated with that response. In fact, he was quite happy. After all, a diamond is always handy, to pay off debts.

But for Bubna, putting it on before the sun hit the skies each day as she dressed for work, was often the best part of her day. It was the happiest part. She didn't have a mirror at home so she would take a minute or even two, just to feel it on her nose. She fell in love with its contours – the jagged edges and how it felt on her skin. Then she would caress the skin around it – some days it felt calloused but most days it felt sensuous to her touch. Since she began wearing the nose stone, she had become immune to the 'emerge' of her neighbours from their shanties each morning as she walked to the train station before light fell. She no longer *really* noticed the queues for the shared bathroom or the teenagers rubbing sleep off their eyes waiting for a squatting space to brush into the solitary drain of their by–lane. Previously the daily sight of these queues would evoke pity in her – for 'her lot'. But now, for her they had just metamorphosed into banal daily queues that lined her way to the main road. And she smiled with other things on her mind. She would invariably remember how she looked in the mirror of the train window the day before and imagine how she would look today.

Today she had worn her favourite maroon sari etched with a gold border. There was nothing to celebrate as such yet she was feeling celebratory. She wondered if anyone would pay her a compliment, but that was for later. For now, she couldn't wait to get on the train, to see how the sparkle of her nose stone against the maroon of her sari looked in the faint train window–mirror.

The train station was its usual self. It smelt of sweat and thousands of people 'put in a hurry' to make a basic living. Bubna's slim frame resiliently jostled through the platform and onto the train. It normally took two to three stations till she could wriggle her way through the pack of people to a train window to watch herself in the mirror that dawn etched on it. The days she could not reach a window before daybreak, her mirror would be gone.

The clamour of people on the train today was as it was every day. The only thing unusual was the glitter of her gold sari border. Her mind too felt the same as every other day. She was again angry about some things her husband had said to her the night before. Just that this time she was happy with herself that she was beginning to fight back. Though she knew no one in her family would be happy about this and most especially her mother was unhappy about her new found 'fighting back' zeal.

'Which man are you seeing, you whore, that you are learning to answer back?' her husband kept pushing her on the waist the night before and asking with the sinister look in his eyes that still scared her despite her growing feistiness with him.

She was generally a feisty lady. In all the six homes she worked in, her employers considered her ways and speak, crude. But with her husband, she was muted. Cowed even. Taking his daily vituperations and occasional drunken beatings, as normal. Part of the territory of being a woman and a wife. She had seen her father do that to her mother. Her uncles to her aunts. Her brother—in—law to her sister. So she understood, from very early on, this was the way.

As the train chugged along, part of her was abusing her husband silently and a bigger part of her dreaming of the man on the paper advertisement plastered above the train windows. She could not read any English but she loved what she saw. A fair, handsome man tenderly holding the hand of a fair, beautiful woman. They were looking into each other's eyes. Smilingly. She somehow felt a loathing for the lady in the advertisement. The lady was wearing a dress accessorized with an ornate diamond necklace and a ring with a teal stone that was at least ten times the size of Bubna's nose stone. Bubna imagined herself as that lady – whom she felt a loathing for because she so wished to be like her. Fair, with a ring. And an off shoulder, turquoise dress. And, above all, a good looking man smiling into 'her' eyes. Is it only fair women who get a man's love, she wondered to herself.

Her musings were suddenly torn apart by blood curdling screams. Brittle screams that cracked with such horror that 'seeing' them was unbearable. The train had just chugged into the next train station. The rest was a sharp, shrieking blur. Rampaging mobs; blood soiled crude knives and sticks; the smell of blood over sweat; the terror of slogans over fear; of destruction over terrified human life.

Bubna tasted blood on her lips. She felt her face, her nose for her nose stone. It was there. She touched it and she felt safe though her fingers slid on the blood on it and on her face. Blood marbled with the sweat of heat and fear.

She bent down and shoved her petite frame under a train seat. She sat there shaking till the rampage abated. All the while she clutched on to her mobile phone as though it was a loved one. When the rampage was over she emerged to bodies strewn across the train compartment, like dead fish floating on a sea. Armani Exchange was writ large on a man's red T–shirt. She wondered if it was a new shirt. A child on her grandmother's lap. Both slouched dead on the train seat. A pink Barbie hairband sat dangling from the grandmother's right fingers. Many stories consumed into one. By terror.

Bubna got off the train, a few stops ahead of the station she needed. She wondered if any of her employers would let her take a shower in their home. She used the maroon of her sari to wipe off the blood on her face and elbows. The blood on her hair she could not see or know of.

She walked all the way back to her third employer's house. She was running late so would not be able to make it to the other two houses she reckoned. Her phone kept ringing and she seemed not to hear it. She just kept walking. When she entered into the flat of her employer, Ahilya, her employer's university going daughter, was nonchalantly changing television channels. In another room her father was also changing television channels between Hindi and English news services to track the violence that had just erupted. A Muslim had allegedly killed a cow, just as an act to insult Hindus. The Hindus stormed lanes, by lanes, trains and buses that passed Muslim *mahallas*[9] seeking revenge. Now it was over to the Muslims to retaliate.

Ahilya, noticing Bubna's blood stained hair, asked, 'What happened?'

Bubna, checked for her nose stone. It was not there. She panicked. She had paid for it herself. Her first gift to herself with her own earnings. That she had kept a secret from everyone.

She went into the kitchen and along its longest wall, taking its support, slouched her back into a squat. And she cried. Bitterly.

All the while, her *saab* was watching the shrill debate on Republic TV. On the main living room television. Giving her tears privacy while the programme debated which politician was on which side and how. The nation wanted to know. But this was being quickly ascertained behind newsrooms, beyond their purview. The stakes were big – the situation had to be capitalised on. Quickly. Vote banks had to be milked. The general election was in the approach.

The small stakes, that of a nose stone, were not part of any debate. Bubna reached for her sari border to wipe her face. A special gold. On a blood darkened maroon sari.

Endnotes

1 Names of protagonists/characters where known have been changed to ensure their anonymity unless they have specifically asked for, and consented to, their real names being used.

2 A children's charity – www.paintourworld.org

3 I felt no existing word better conveyed the feeling of 'being cared for', hence I've coined the word 'caree'.

4 This story is based on my visit to the island of Suomenlinna that is a boat ride from the Finnish capital Helsinki.

5 An Indian sweet dish made with carrots, nuts and clarified butter.

6 Based on a true story narrated to me.

7 Aarti is part of the Hindu ritual of prayer. It is an offering of fire (light) made to the deities to the tune of specific devotional songs. This offering is usually made at the end of the prayer sequence.

8 Based on a true story.

9 areas